Dedicated to football fans everywhere.

First published in Great Britain in 1991 by
Paper Plane Publishing Ltd
Forge House
Forge Lane
Cradley Heath
West Midlands
B64 5AL

Acknowledgements

All the players, managers and coaches I've worked with. Despite what I've said about them in this book, I hope we can still be friends.
My wife Alice, Paul Miller, David Instone, Phil Walder, Bob Hall, Jasper Carrott, Stuart Pearce and especially Bob Harrison.

ISBN 1 871872 05 7
Paper Plane Publishing Ltd

Printed in Great Britain by Cradley Print Ltd

Illustrations by *Milly*

Picture Acknowledgements Coventry Evening Telegraph, Birmingham Post & Mail, Action Images and The Express & Star

The Author –
Brian 'HARRY' Roberts

Displaying the uncanny sense of timing that was to be the hallmark of his career as a professional footballer, a young Brian Roberts joined Coventry City at the same time as a police murderer known as Harry Roberts was making the surname infamous.

Not unnaturally his new team-mates christened him with the nick-name 'Harry'. Unfortunate perhaps, but it suited him so much that it stuck long after the notoriety of the case had subsided, and today few people know the blond haired fullback as Brian.

From his earliest days as a professional footballer, his wit in the dressing room was well known to his team-mates. It was opened to a wider audience when he started writing an amusing column in the Birmingham Sports Argus and it is this that led to him being approached to write a humourous book about football and his experiences in the game.

Now 36 'Harry' is as keen about football as he was as a raw Highfield Road apprentice. His enthusiasm hasn't dulled and his wit is sharper than ever.

Contents

Introduction

Why on earth have I written a book, you're probably asking. It's a question I've been regularly asked, especially by my publisher. I suppose it's one of life's unanswerable questions, like: why does a light-bulb always go when it's too dark to replace it? Why can't you ever find a needle apart from when you're walking across the room bare-footed? Why do Oxford and Cambridge always get to the final of the Boat Race? Why, when you're not one hundred per cent on match-days, do you come up against a whippet wearing Reeboks?

Despite the fact that I am having to consider joining Wolves' President Sir Jack Hayward as a tax exile in The Bahamas – due to the massive advance royalty payments from this book – I can honestly say that I didn't write it for the money.

Nor did I write it to disprove the popular misconception that a footballer's vocabulary is limited to clichés like "I'm over the moon, Brian," "Sick as a parrot," and "We woz robbed."

Neither did I write it to expose the festering depravity and corruption that is rife in the game, because I haven't managed to find any.

No, what really motivated me was my desire to have a bit of fun. As I look back at everything I have achieved over two decades in the game – and what an enjoyable two minutes that gave me – the most consistent factor has not been my level of performance, but the humour surrounding the sport.

A lot of people said I could never do it but I don't know the meaning of the word failure. Mind you, there are a lot of words I don't know the meaning of.

I couldn't let this introduction go without a mention for Paul Gascoigne. There, I've mentioned him. That should sell a few thousand copies. And, finally, a word of thanks to my boss at Wolves, Graham Turner, without whose help this publication would not have been possible. His generosity in giving me so many Saturday afternoons off this season has been invaluable!

1. A New Start

I felt lower than a limbo dancer's backside when I left Birmingham City in the summer of 1990 and found myself on the dole for the first time in my life. I felt shattered that Real Madrid had been told of my availability and had still not bothered to pick up the phone.

I thought it was probably the end of my career and so I took a look around at what I had achieved in the game. That didn't take long. Other players have trophies all over their mantlepiece, I have a bowl of fruit and a layer of dust.

I thought about launching a private lottery with entries invited to the Brian Roberts Caribbean Cruise Fund. I also considered joining Athletics Anonymous - an organisation in which members think about taking up a competitive sport, meet in a bar every month and order enough drinks to satisfy them until the urge goes off.

For two weeks I had been a government unemployment statistic, when I received a very strange phone call. My wife took it and thought it might be from St. Andrew's, but we realised it couldn't be as the caller hadn't reversed the charges.

She said the chap on the other end refused to give his name. That worried me straightaway. Who could it be? Obviously someone who hated publicity. Jeremy Beadle, Anneka Rice and Paul Gascoigne sprung to mind, but it wasn't any of them.

An unfamiliar voice said: "I'm not at liberty at the moment to say who it is, but bear with me. Do you live near a motorway?" I thought it was the A.A. (not George Best's lot, the others). Fair enough, I knew I might be heading for a breakdown but not the type the Automobile Association could have helped with!

I replied that, if it meant a job, I did live near a motorway. So close, in fact, that I had a hard shoulder instead of a drive and cones in my borders, rather than flowers. "Good," he said. "Is it true that you have had a free transfer from Birmingham City?" I thought: 'Ay, ay, it's the taxman.'

"Whatever you do," I was told, "don't sign for anybody else until you have heard from me again. I've watched you play and I've been impressed" (muffled laughter). I said: "Heard from who? I don't know who you are." He replied: "I'm not at liberty to say at the moment." I said: "Can you give me a clue?" "Yes, it's not Lionel Bloody Blair." The one revelation he did make was that he was ringing on behalf of a club in a higher division than the one I had left, which narrowed it down to 44 teams.

With no prospects, no future and no money, (at this point, sympathetic types can send their cheques to B. Roberts Esq, c/o Little House on the Prairie) at least it was a ray of hope. I put the phone down, told my wife I had no idea who it was and subsequently dismissed the conversation as a wind-up by one of my former team-mates.

Up to this point, I had kept in trim by running three miles a day. Trouble was that come the first Sunday night, I was 21 miles away and had missed the last bus home. Encouraged and intrigued by the call, I stepped up my roadwork and continued to mull over who the club could be by going through the First and Second Divisions. Did Alex Ferguson have a Black Country accent? Had someone given George Graham my ex-directory number?

There was no follow-up call for some time and I began to think more about responding to some of the whispers I had heard about Fourth Division and non-League clubs being interested. I had plenty of irons in the fire, but none of them seemed to be getting hot. I was becoming desperate. I was down to my last £100,000 in the bank, the swimming pool was about to be filled in and one of the Porsches had been repossessed off the drive. But things weren't all black. The wife still had her coal-round in the afternoons and supplemented our income with wrestling bouts at night.

Then the mystery voice came back, just as I was watching Harold and Madge go into a clinch in Neighbours. Would I agree to a chat the following Monday morning? I checked my diary, said I would put Cloughie and Kenny Dalglish off until another day and said yes. I was in a state of elation and just about to put the phone down when I realised I still didn't know who the mystery caller was.

"Oh yes," he said. "Meet us at Molineux. Graham Turner will be waiting there." I couldn't believe it.

Wolverhampton Wanderers wanted me. The best club in the world and the best manager (I could creep for England,

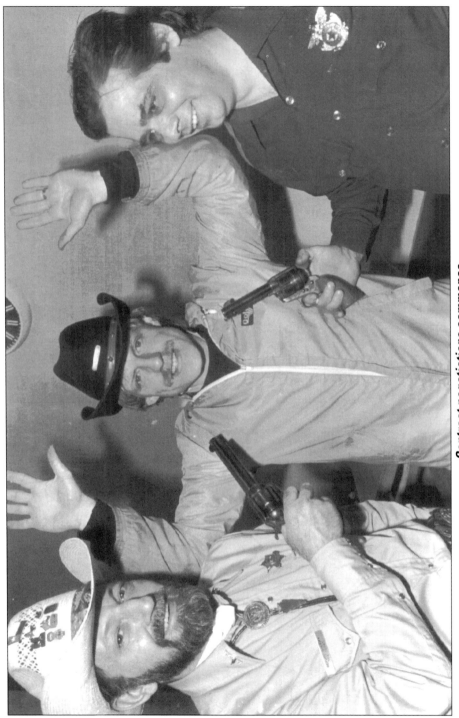

Contract negotiations commence

me) but with a ground like the city of Coventry during the blitz. Some of those stands were even older than the action photos in Garry Pendrey's private collection. But I was in with a chance of employment again, doing a job I loved.

2. Wolves Pre-season

Pre-season training, in my first few weeks at Wolves, went so well I felt I was 33 all over again. I had played well in the warm-up matches (always a bad sign!) and took in my stride all the running up and down the sand dunes on our summer trip to Anglesey.

We were on our travels again when we flew to Northern Ireland to play Glenavon — the club Wolves winger Robbie Dennison played for before his career went downhill — and also took on Southampton, Shrewsbury, Chelsea, Arsenal and Swansea in friendlies. I missed only two of the games and had proved there was life in the old dog yet.

The pitches still hadn't lost their early-season greenness and the players still hadn't kissed goodbye to their carefully nurtured sun-tans, when the news came that left me feeling lower than a footballer's IQ. I switched on the TV and heard that the gaffer had splashed out £500,000 on Kevin Ashley from Birmingham. I had nothing against this transaction, except that Kevin was also a full-back and left my chances of retaining the No. 2 shirt about as strong as Oliver Reed's will to say no to the offer of a quick drink before breakfast.

Half a million quid, I ask you! What sort of future did that present for me — a free-transfer pick-up from the same club? It was all very well being described as a good dressing-room influence but I wanted to get out of it and on to the pitch occasionally.

Kevin agreed his move to Molineux on the Wednesday and the gaffer called me into his office on the Thursday. 'This is it', I thought. 'You've had a good run, Harry, but this is the end of the line.'

I walked in and the boss said: "Sit down, Harry. No, not there, you're hurting my legs. Use a chair. Now you've obviously heard I've bought Kevin Ashley. But don't let it worry you. Okay, he may be, and always will be, 13 years younger than you and it cost us £500,000 to sign him ahead of other clubs. But don't worry — I've bought him for the future."

Worry? I was inconsolable. The future started that very next Saturday with a game against West Ham at Upton Park and I was sure to be for the chop. But the gaffer said I was in the team on merit and would stay there as long as I kept cleaning his car.

I was so relieved, I got up straightaway and made for the door. But he stopped me in my tracks by saying: "How about an extension?" I replied: "To tell you the truth, boss, we won't be having any more family, so three bedrooms are ample. But thanks, anyway." He said: "No, an extension to your contract."

I couldn't believe it. Here I was, a 34-year-old just about to be replaced by a 21-year-old and I was being offered a new contract to soften the blow. Did I want a new contract! Does a donkey like strawberries? Does an Irishman like Guinness? Does Steve Bull like scoring goals?

After I'd bitten the gaffer's hand off, muttering "Thank you, boss, thank you, thank you very much," I retreated to the door as quickly as possible, hoping I could escape before he came to his senses. But he called me back by asking: "Isn't there something you've forgotten?" I said: "No, your car is cleaned and polished and it's waiting on the forecourt for you." He said: "No, not that, money. Do you want some more money?"

I pinched myself again and set about negotiating the pay-rise for the contract extension I couldn't believe I was getting. He asked me what I thought I was worth. I told him, he laughed and said: "I've already got your phone number" – and promptly halved my evaluation. We quickly shook on it (actually, I'd been shaking all the time I was in there) and went our separate ways.

Shortly afterwards, club secretary Keith Pearson confronted me and told me there was a technical hitch which meant I couldn't have a pay rise in the second year of my contract. I would have to have it now. "Bloody red tape," I moaned — and left the room feeling higher than Niall Quinn's dandruff.

Before the West Ham game, I said to myself over and over again: "I'm going to justify the gaffer's faith in me, have a blinder and make it impossible for him to drop me — even for a £500,000 youngster. In three months time, Kevin Ashley will realise he has no future here, will discover that I will play until I'm 40 and will ask for a transfer."

I was partly right. I started the match in the No. 2 shirt, Kevin was on the subs' bench and I had a storming game. Then a sniper in the crowd whom Ash had hired caught me a painful blow and I went down like a lead balloon. Actually, it was my hamstring. My West Ham-string, you might say. I missed the game at Swindon three days later, Kevin came in and I faced a long haul back.

I faced another stretch on the treatment table, a position you become accustomed to as a professional footballer. But, in spite of my injury, I had to consider myself fortunate – at the age of 34 – to be looking forward to two years at a new club, playing the game I love.

3. The Beginning

I was born on November 6, 1955. On a Sunday. Apparently, all kind and good-natured people are. I hardly needed to wait for a club to come and sign me a decade and a half later. I could nearly have formed a team of my own as there were nine brothers and sisters in our squad.

Mum had a hearing problem. Just before the bedroom light went out last thing at night, Dad would say: "Are you tired, or what?" She would look puzzled and say: "What?" And that was it, another one on the way.

Mum and Dad were poor. They lived in a mid-terrace slum just outside wedlock. And the neighbourhood was rough. The Alsatians used to go round in pairs and even the rainbows were in black and white. The walls of our house were so thin, the bloke next door could dip his bread in our gravy.

Grandad lived with us for a while and worked as a rag-and-bone man. The second-hand clothes came in handy but it was no fun going to school dressed as a Japanese general.

Dad was a professional carol singer. For 11 months of the year, we would starve but, come December, we would always have something to sing about. The spirit of Christmas was a bit thin on the ground, though. He once gave me an empty box as a present and told me it was an Action Man Deserter. Yes, we learned to appreciate boxes in those days. In fact, I used to get one round the ear most days. One year, we were all crammed in the sitting room watching a cut-out of a TV set from a newspaper when we heard this almighty bang. Dad rushed out of the room and then raced back in to give us the sad news. Santa Claus had committed suicide. Out came last year's box again.

I used to think my Dad was going to be a policeman as he was always helping them with their enquiries. At one stage, he went off on holiday on his own. For five years. At Dartmoor. He even had letters after his name, G.B.H. My Mum said they stood for Gorgeous Big Hunk. I said I would follow in his footsteps, it would be a crime if I didn't. She said it would be a crime if I did. Anyway, I stopped having brothers and sisters for a while.

Once a month, Mum and I would get the bus into Manchester Picadilly and then catch the coach down to Dartmoor. What a journey! It was great fun the first couple of times, then it became a right chore. I remember wishing he would move to a 'hotel' nearer home. I did not think much of the one he

To this day I still get my sisters' hand-me-downs

was in. They never used to let the guests out to get a tan. It must have been one of those twin-centre holidays, though, because he finally moved to a place in Manchester. I can't remember the name of it but it certainly had some strange ways!

It wasn't an easy childhood and I quickly discovered I had to fend for myself. I learned to swim in the local canal, which wasn't too difficult once I'd fought my way out of the sack. I later used the community baths, although the drought was so bad one year that they had to close lanes six and seven.

Money was tight but the hairdresser came round four times a month. Once to give us all a short-back-and-sides, three more times to try to get us to pay.

So, as you can see, I had the perfect background to achieve my late father's wish — for me not to work. Accordingly, I set my sights on a career as a professional footballer.

During my long and undistinguished career I have been privy to the funny, sometimes downright hilarious side of the game. And, in this book, I attempt, through my own experiences, to take you inside it's funny world.

As Oscar Wilde (or was it Jack?) once said: "People are at their funniest when trying to be serious." Or at least he would have done if he had played professional football.

4. Sky Blues Apprenticeship

Football can be a cruel game at times, especially if you're a young apprentice at a club where traditions die hard. At Coventry, like in the printing industry, it was an age-old custom for all the youngsters to be 'given the treatment' when they first reported for training.

People in other walks of life have been arrested and convicted for less, but the 'blacking up' ceremony at Highfield Road went on for years without the knowledge of Amnesty International. The unfortunate victim would be stripped naked, given two minutes to go and hide in some protected part of the training ground and then pursued by the rest of the players armed with black boot polish (or dubbin if times were good), vaseline and scrubbing brushes.

The rest of the story doesn't really need any explaining, but, if you're still mystified as to what happened then, let me enlighten you. The screaming unfortunate was inevitably caught, smeared all over his body and hair (no great problem if his name was Greg Downs) with the aforementioned materials, then painfully buffed up with brushes. I'm sure Coventry City is where the phrase 'In the buff' was conjured up and I would lay my last dollar that Cynthia Payne got the idea for her dinner parties from what went on in our strange world.

At the time of my own initiation, I learned one or two lessons, which, unfortunately, came too late to help me. The first was not to make it difficult for the bloodthirsty pack to find you. If you did, you copped the blackening twice as bad and your private parts never regained their natural colour.

The other golden rule was not to succumb to the obvious temptation of jumping in the shower straight after the dastardly deed. If you did, the water and soap seemed to cement everything rather than wash it off. It was much better to scrape the offending substances off with a knife first.

When I was introduced to this more dubious side of our noble game, the tea-lady came out to watch, presumably for a giggle. Whenever I went to eat in the canteen afterwards, she always served me bigger helpings. I don't know whether she was impressed by the eyeful she'd had or whether she thought my physique was sadly lacking!

Now, this initiation was all very routine for most youngsters but the passing of the years in post-war Britain has led to a more cosmopolitan society and more races. In other words, we would occasionally plan to 'blacken up' one of the lads and then remember that nature had beaten us to it.

One of the first such players - a young man born in Birmingham but of West Indian descent - was on the hit-list this one day when we stumbled on the idea of whitening him instead. Out came the gloss, a full litre can of the stuff.

We took quite a shine to him afterwards and the finish was so good we called him Matt. Unfortunately, he didn't make it in football but I'm told his (mis) treatment gave him the idea of embarking on a thriving painting and decorating business. Sorry to gloss over the details but I've got mixed emulsions about the whole issue.

Football clubs, of course, are breeding grounds for high jinks and practical jokes and Ernie Hunt was very much the Clown Prince in my early days at Coventry. He once reduced me to an embarrassed heap during one of my extra duties as I carried the tea-tray generously loaded up by our canteen lady, Joyce, to manager Gordon Milne's office.

Because I had my hands full as I approached the door, I asked Ernie if he would give it a gentle knock for me. Gentle knock? He nearly banged a hole through the wood with his fist and then swiftly made his escape. But not before, at precisely the moment the handle started to turn from inside, taking advantage of my helplessness by pulling my shorts down round my ankles. By the time I offered the tray to Gordon Milne and Ron Wylie, Ernie was nowhere to be seen but I was naked from the waist down and very red-faced. Gordon saw the joke (if you know what I mean) and said: "I don't remember ordering sausage" before ending my ordeal by taking away the tray and its contents.

As a winder-up of some repute, Ernie Hunt inevitably found the boot on the other foot at times, notably when comedian Freddie Starr paid us a visit at our training ground one hot summer's day. Seeing a big circular sprinkler in operation, Freddie meticulously placed various items of Ernie's clothes in such a way that they would be right in the firing line as the contraption rotated.

Freddie did the decent thing and let Ernie know when he

Fashion Victims 1972 (By the way, I'm the good looking one on the right of the front row)

was switching the water on. But shuttle runs weren't poor Ernie's strong point and the rest of we players were in fits of laughter as he displayed the uncanny knack of arriving at each garment just after a huge spray of water!

● ● ● ● ●

So how did I come to be a professional footballer and, more importantly, what was it that possessed Coventry City to give me my big chance?

Of all the people who influenced, advised and helped me in my formative years, I can certainly say my father wasn't one of them. I didn't have his backing in any way. That earlier stuff about him being imprisoned during my childhood wasn't an example of the Roberts sense of humour running wild. It was true. He was an old rogue, all right.

He had been a boxer in his early days and wanted me to follow him into the ring. Sure enough, I went training and fighting at the gym for a while and, when I returned home bruised and sometimes bleeding, he would say: "Boxing's a great sport isn't it, son? Better than that namby-pamby game, football." Deep down, I knew I couldn't box kippers and pledged to follow my own instincts rather than his.

I had a reasonable schoolboy career with Yew Tree High in Wythenshawe, Manchester Boys and local team Mercer Celtic - and had been spotted by the father of Graham Paddon, a scout for Coventry. But it was my school sports-teacher, John Thompson, who was instrumental in getting me to Coventry, for whom he later worked as a scout in the north.

John was there the day I, and three other youngsters being signed, were treated to lunch in the presence of then manager Noel Cantwell. My Dad was there, too, but he never came to see me play either before or after. It was the poshest 'do' I'd ever been to and he was the only one not wearing a tie. In fact, he never wore a tie in his life - only after he died. Mum and me finally had our way and smartened him up while his body was lying in the coffin with the lid about to be closed.

He may not have been the best father one could have had but he had been determined not to miss my big moment - the day I signed for Coventry in a Liverpool hotel in 1971. In fact Mum has still got some of the hotel's silver today.

I was glad to leave Manchester and break into a new environment, although I was subsequently so homesick that I used to cry myself off to sleep and go back to see my family at every opportunity - sometimes just for a night at a time.

Leeds, Manchester City and Manchester United had been interested in signing me but I opted for Coventry because I thought I had more chance of breaking through via the youth team at a smaller club. Dennis Mortimer, Bobby Parker and Mick McGuire had done that at Highfield Road, so I, Ray Murphy and two cousins called Cahill (Paul and Tony) had a definite goal as we moved starry-eyed into the big world of professional football.

Life at Coventry wasn't easy, although, as one of nine children, I was used to the cramped living quarters that came with sharing the club hostel with 13 or 14 other apprentices. An Irish couple, Eva and Jim Shirley, ran the lodgings, which were in an area of the city notorious for prostitution, and knew only part of what was going on when their backs were turned.

Mick Ferguson, a year and a good two feet above me in the youth development programme, was not against the idea of waking me up occasionally with a bucket of cold water and I once matched fire with fire by beating up a team-mate called George Scott, a Geordie who had been giving me a hard time. George, an intelligent lad who later went off to college or university, went up considerably in my estimations for declining to report the difference of opinion – and I was sufficiently respected afterwards never to be picked on again.

In football's evolutionary pattern, I probably then picked on younger players as I climbed the ladder leading towards the first team. That was the sort of competitive atmosphere we lived in. We were young lads trying to make our way in the game and trying to show we could look after ourselves at the same time.

On another occasion, we kidded a colleague that we were sneaking out one night to do a bank job. So convincing were we with our patter and so menacing with our threats that we had him practising the line "I didn't see anything, honest" over and over again in preparation for what we told him could be a grilling from the police.

These high jinks were born out of boredom. We were virtually living on top of each other and there was bound to be friction. Needless to say, not many of us actually made it. In fact from my year's intake of apprentices, I was the only one. And I hovered on the verge of being discarded for so long it was May 8, 1975, before I finally signed as a pro.

It was on that day that three of us had to go in one by one to learn our fate. I was kept on, the other two fell by the wayside. I didn't have to ask how they had got on when they emerged from manager Gordon Milne's office. They were crying their eyes out. I tried to reassure them that there were 91 other League clubs and one of them would take them on. But they didn't, and I've never seen or heard of my two contemporaries from that day to this. But there's a fair chance they haven't heard of me either.

5. The Family

Isn't there a saying that goes something like: Behind every successful man, there's a good woman? Well, I offer this slight amendment: Behind every successful man, there's a bully.

Yes, my beloved Alice and I have now been happily and faithfully married for 15 years.

I know people will find it hard to believe that I'm old enough to have a family and responsibilities. And they will probably be at a loss to understand why, with my young-free-and-single appearance and boyish good looks, I turned my back on the bachelor life and decided to settle down.

Well, I can tell you, there's not much fun in being chased from party to party and bedroom to bedroom by adoring females. At least that's what Eric Gates told me.

No. I tied the knot at an early age to escape all that attention. I never wanted to be rich anyway. And I've got a weakness for red-heads. Not red hair, just red heads.

Alice is a Londonderry girl with typical Irish looks - scarlet hair with moustache and nose to match. Her family moved to England and settled in the Coventry area when she was ten, her father running the Mercer's Arms pub right next to Coventry's Highfield Road ground.

I accidentally strayed into the pub one afternoon thinking it was an art gallery and was smitten by a sight so lovely it took my breath away: a long, cool pint of lager on the counter! The colleen who had served it caught my eye too. I knew she was the one for me, the way she could arm-wrestle a gorilla and pull a pint of Guinness at the same time, and she was so clever! All her tattoos were spelt correctly.

I couldn't believe it when our eyes met across the dusty pool table or, a few drambuie-shandies later, when she smiled at me. 'What the heck,' I thought. 'Go for it, Harry.' Casual as you like, I asked: "Do you come here often?" And she whispered back in that sensuous Irish lilt: "I live here, you prat." It's funny how things stick in your mind, isn't it? I knew from that moment that this was the girl I was going to marry - and not just because her Dad had a pub!

Up to this point, I had only seen her top half - lips like petals (bicycle 'petals') and teeth like stars (they came out at night). She stepped out from behind the bar to collect the empties and she looked a picture. Mind you, I had seen better legs

Tying the knot: Getting married brought a lump to my throat

hanging out of a sparrow's nest and she had the sort of calves that only a cow could love.

Courting was a bit embarrassing. Alice earned quite a bit more than my princely £7.50 a week and, on her evening off, was able to make a proper night-out of it. Unfortunately, I had to be back at the Coventry hostel by 10.30pm and she used to walk me to the door to keep me out of temptation's way. Which, sad to say, she succeeded in doing.

We married in the summer of 1976, which proved to be one of the hottest on record. Shrewdly, I chose to wear a woollen three-piece suit and a velvet tie with a knot that could have been used to help berth the QE2. I could barely move my head, which was a pity because I longed to crane my neck sideways and look at Alice. She looked stunning in her sequined dungarees and designer clogs. Her mother's long service in the bricklaying trade had come in useful with her make-up and she looked a delight stumbling down the aisle.

The ceremony itself went without a hitch and, after a two-year courtship, we were finally man and wife. I had tried to surprise her with the honeymoon by booking a round-the-world cruise. But she said: "Can't we go somewhere else?" Then I suggested Devon and Cornwall - but she wasn't too impressed when she realised I was going to Devon and she to Cornwall.

Eventually, I put my foot down with a firm hand and booked us on a Med special to Majorca. I had booked us into the best hotel money could lend. It was so posh! Alice, I'm afraid, was a little out of her depth. At dinner, she tried to order a faggot-and-peas batch with a pint of cider. I told her you had lager with faggots and peas, not cider. I took over in an effort to help her out of her embarrassment. "We'll both have the Chateaubriand," I said. "How would you like it, Alice?" "You know I only drink Aspispewalotti," she replied, "so forget the wine and order us something to eat." I gave up!

The honeymoon was a bit of a flop and we couldn't wait to get home and start a family right away. Two years later, first son Mark made his entry into God's world at 7lb 8oz. Three-

Wife of Brian

month colic, teething troubles, sleepless nights . . . I had the lot! To catch up on lost sleep, we decided to wait five years for Roberts Jnr. Mark II - and, when he arrived, he was completely different. He would sleep all night and lie on his back on the floor shouting 'Feed me' as soon as he knew how. Very much like his Dad, actually.

It was mutually decided, by Alice, that that would be the sum total of our contribution to the population boom. As a result, she booked me in for a vasectomy and I was in the waiting room with only a paper gown to protect my dignity before I realised a vasectomy wasn't the latest model Ford. I asked the surgeon if I would be able to ride a bike afterwards. He told me I would, to which I expressed great admiration for the advancement of medical science. I could never ride one before.

Ten minutes later, with my clothes in one hand and the remnants of my manhood in the other, it was all over. I immediately went off for an audition with the Coventry Boys' Choir and started to contemplate the benefits of the operation. Next day, I asked the doctor if there was any way he could take away the pain but keep the swelling, alas no. But he told me to keep wearing the truss. I said: "No problem, what good is a marriage if there's no truss?"

Both Mark and Paul have turned out to be good-looking lads and I've since been back to the midwife to check they're mine. They are both articulate and intelligent, so I've had to resign myself to the fact that they won't become footballers.

Seriously, Mark loves football, is captain of his school team and plays every available minute of the day. He would rather play soccer than go out with girls (where did I go wrong?) but Paul is a real John Travolta, a brilliant song-and-dance man. Whatever the two of them do in life, I just hope they make enough money to one day keep their old Mum and Dad in the luxury Steve Bull's accustomed to.

6. Goals I Have Scored

This is the section in which I could have rambled on and on, barely pausing for breath or to consider that important virtue called modesty. But, because of those well-known publishing world enemies, time and space, I've decided to write about only two of the goals I've scored in my glittering career as a Football League player.

I will one day, however, go happily into retirement reflecting on the hundreds, nay thousands, of mere tap-ins I've laid on for those fortunate enough to have been around to play alongside me.

Fortunately, all my goals came in the same season, so it wasn't too difficult picking my way through the record books to pinpoint when they were. And, okay, there were only two of them - both for Coventry - but what beauties they were.

Observers of international repute reckoned my first was worth the ten years' wait for its quality and execution. I can't remember all the details but it was against West Ham at Upton Park on December 11, 1982, there was 78 per cent humidity, the temperature was 62.5 degrees and there was a north to north easterly gently sweeping the ground and rustling the fringes of the 19,321 crowd, the names and addresses of whom are available on request.

I was playing at left-back and had had scrambled eggs on lightly browned toast for lunch. It was approaching half-time and we were leading 1-0 thanks to a Mark Hateley tap-in from a cross by . . . (see above). Now, don't ask me why I did it. Call it sixth sense, call it destiny, call it goalscorers' intuition, but I made this off-the-ball forward run down the left. All the opposition saw me but, as usual, nobody bothered, it was only Harry on one of his misadventures out of the half he was most comfortable in — his own! Danny Thomas had the ball on the right and was taking on players and beating them in precisely the manner I'd taught him.

Still no-one picked me up as I foraged even further into the territory in which I normally developed a nose-bleed. Not this time, though. Danny crossed, it eluded everyone, but not Harry Roberts. He, I mean I, met it on the volley when it finally came down, and everyone took the usual course of action. The crowd ducked, manager Dave Sexton started yelling Zen Buddhism at me from the dug-out and my team-mates turned round in readiness for the ensuing goal-kick. But a strange thing happened on this occasion.

Instead of disappearing up West Ham High Street, the ball

arrowed a glorious path towards the top corner of the net. Phil Parkes, who was at the peak of his magnificent career, was left floundering - big scorch marks showing on his glove where he had foolishly attempted to get his hand behind it. I was a goalscorer and, once the shock had worn off and I realised it was no sweet dream, I celebrated in the time-honoured way, doing a lap of the pitch in record time.

After the game, I had a word with Phil and commiserated with him. We both knew he was finished from that moment. If I could beat him, it was time to hang up his peaked cap. Sure enough, the public ridicule that followed was too much for him and his career went all downhill from then on.

As for me, it was just one of those one-in-a-million cases when the ball went exactly where I aimed it. It was later said that it was the best goal ever seen at the famous Upton Park ground. It was me who said it, but it could just have easily have been my wife Alice or one of our two sons.

'Hotshot Harry,' the scourge of tens of thousands of spectators the length and breadth of the country who had foolishly stood within 20 yards either side of the goalposts, had struck. No more would I be on the end of cruel jibes about unsuspecting pigeons gliding across serene skies then being re-routed to their maker by a blow from a white leather spherical object somehow propelled into near-orbit. No more jibes about inscriptions on headstones of tombs bearing the remains of blackbirds who had considered themselves safe when flying in the slipstream of roaring jets. No more jibes about God looking down on his slain feathered creatures and saying of their passing-away: "I can't say whether it was a cross or a shot, but I can say most definitely that Harry's back in town."

Dave Sexton couldn't let the golden moment go unrecognised. He had a consignment of 'I saw Harry score' badges struck up and distributed among a disbelieving public. Actually, they were snapped up in double-quick time by local dealers, who obviously saw them as rare collectors' items. Some of the badges were snapped up by youngsters, who I was appalled to hear were subsequently beaten to within an inch of their

lives by parents yelling at them not to tell lies. "You CAN'T have seen Harry score - take that!"

My next goal (or should it be my last goal?) was against Norwich City at Highfield Road in the FA Cup. It was a much simpler affair. I went on an underlap down the right wing (it should have been an overlap but I'm not big enough) and Steve Hunt played the ball into my path. I had one touch, then wham! The power of the shot was such that the keeper had time to put down his woodbine, finish tying his laces, adjust his cap and then turn his thoughts to plucking it out of the air. What he hadn't bargained for was the vicious spin I had put on the ball. I hadn't meant to, I had just mis-hit it as usual. It squirmed out of his hands and, quicker than it takes me to close the door on a Jehovah's Witness, I poked in the rebound.

As chance would have it, I nearly scored in every game that season - I nearly scored against Arsenal, I nearly scored against Tottenham, I nearly scored against Everton and I . . . nearly always tell the truth! Actually, those two goals put me off wanting to score for the rest of my life.

I quickly found that all that kissing and hugging lark wasn't really my scene at all, particularly with some of the lipstick that was popular among the lads at the time. And there was one player, who shall remain nameless unless I receive a good offer from one of the Sunday papers, who, seizing his chance, tried to indulge in a little French kissing.

I studied his behaviour for quite a while after that unnerving experience and noticed that he was always first in the kissing queue after goals. Even those scored by opposition players! And another thing: I thought it was customary to hold your OWN private parts in the defensive wall at free-kicks. Yes, he worried me so much that I vowed there and then that I would never score again and I've proved true to my word. In fact, I never went over the half-way line again, just in case one of somebody else's shots hit me and went in.

7. Injuries

I'm often asked what the biggest fear is in the life of a professional footballer. Well, I can tell you. It isn't Lou Macari asking you to nip down to the book-ies to put a bet on.

Nor Vinny Jones standing in your vicinity at a corner-kick and seeing how hard he needs to put the squeeze on before he brings the tears to your eyes.

No, the biggest fear is serious injury. No matter how hardened a professional or how fearless you are, the sight and even thought of a player sprawled out on the turf with his knee-cap facing one corner-flag and his toes facing the opposite one is enough to churn your stomach.

It's not the hard tacklers you worry about. They, by and large, are the fair ones. It's the ones who go over the top or go in late that cause the flutters. The ones who dive in when they have no chance of getting the ball and no chance of getting injured themselves. In other words, the cheats and the cowards.

I've seen a fair few of these characters in my time and, sadly, one or two have helped shorten the careers of more honest pros. Fortunately, for every one of this nature, there are half a dozen in the hard-but-fair category - men like Ron 'Chopper' Harris, Norman Hunter, George Curtis, Stuart Pearce and Keith Downing.

They are football's answer to the Scud missile. You know when they're coming at you but there's sod all you can do about it. But they're also gentlemen and, if they should accidentally cause any part of your anatomy to become detached from the main torso, they will help you look for it in the mud afterwards.

I'm sure any fan can look at his favourite team, past or present, and single out just such a player whom they have great affinity with. One who is respected and feared by opponents. And, when two of these hard-men come face-to-face, it's enough to make the floodlight pylons shudder.

I once remember Coventry facing Chelsea and the aforementioned Stuart Pearce stepping into the arena with Graham Roberts in gladiatoral combat. Being defenders on opposing sides, they didn't come into contact much, then the ball broke about 15 yards in between them midway through the second half. A hush fell over the ground. Something had to give.

Get your nose out of my paper Snoz!

Pearce lunged in, Roberts put every ounce of his weight behind his challenge and the two produced a colossal collision. As it happened, Stuart came out with the ball, passed to me and I passed it straight to a Chelsea player. Some things never change.

Graham Roberts, meanwhile, was lying in a pile on the turf, not so much injured as dazed and winded. The way you or I would react if we had just encountered Mike Tyson on a bad day. I spoke to Stuart after the game and congratulated him on the tackle. He shrugged off the compliment and confided that the challenge had hurt him like hell. It was just that his pride wouldn't let him show it. He had bravely carried on, obviously feeling groggy. He must have been. Otherwise, he would never have passed to me!

A lot of players will say they hate playing against Stuart Pearce. I hated playing WITH him. He was such a strong, intimidating opponent that a lot of wingers would face him for 20 painful minutes, then see good sense and swap flanks to take me on. I remember Louie Donowa doing just that for Norwich against us once. He was having a great season but one crunching tackle from Stuart and he was over to my side quicker than it takes Ron Atkinson to change clubs. I can tell you: I've enhanced the reputations of a few players in that way in my time.

My first serious injury was sustained in a League game against Liverpool (what a name-dropper!). Our keeper, Jim Blyth, rolled the ball out to me, which, I remember thinking, was a bit odd as I was on the substitutes' bench at the time.

Seriously, I was playing at right-back and I controlled it (yes, seriously). Normally, I trap a ball further than most players can kick it. The feat obviously went to my head because I made the mistake of trying to dribble round the nearest Liverpool player. The crowd may have been impressed at this, but Graeme Souness wasn't.

He obviously saw me as the greatest threat to his side that day and, well, let's just say, I was soon flat out in agony and my ankle was doing a Chaplin impression. The one consolation was that the game was being televised later that night and, as I was being carried off to hospital, I made a mental note to ring the wife and ask her to video my brave stretcher-bound departure.

As I was helped to the dressing-room, I realised it was worse than I had at first thought. My new sky blue sock had a ladder in it! Fortunately, the stretcher-bearers were skilled in the new medical field (Stockingontomie) and fitted me with a new one.

I was rushed to hospital where I was obviously recognised straightaway because, seven hours later, a doctor came to see me. He said he didn't realise I had a beard. I said I hadn't when I came in.

As it happened, I got home just in time for Match of the Day and was able to shift myself sufficiently to press the 'Record' button on the video. I needn't have bothered. Much to my disgust, my grimaces and other facial contortions - the ones I had been practising for just such an occasion - were totally shielded from the cameras by four ambulancemen, all smiling towards the lens and mouthing the words: "Hello Mum!"

My ankle wasn't actually broken, just severely sprained. And I was so badly missed on the field that we only beat Liverpool 1-0!

The other serious injury that springs to my mind came when I was playing many years later for Birmingham in a Sunday lunchtime home game against West Brom. I actually played on with a broken leg and, to compound the irony of my problems as we lost 1-0, my former team Coventry knocked Leeds out of the FA Cup on the same day, at Hillsborough, to reach Wembley for the first time.

It wasn't that I was jealous. After all, I had been to Wembley myself. I backed the dog in trap six but, unfortunately, the jockey fell off on the first bend.

Anyway, the Sky Blues were off to the twin towers and I was off to hospital - eventually. I've always said that if you're going to break a leg, get a mate to do it. I chose Paul (Jack the Giant) Dyson, another of my old Highfield Road buddies. He had watched me take the ball round two of his Albion colleagues and, once he had stopped laughing, came across to make sure he wasn't the third.

'Harry's never done this before, so why should he start now?' seemed to be his thinking as he raced across like a steam-train and buffeted me clean off the rails.

I had forgotten he had legs the length of a ladder. It was a perfectly fair challenge, although I later purchased the match video just in case I had enough of a claim to take him to court. I didn't. I didn't have a leg to stand on.

I lay there motionless on the ground, doing my impression of an Irishman on a Saturday night. Peter Henderson, the physio, came rushing on and then slowed down to a gentle trot and lit his pipe when he saw it was only me. He checked that Paul's boot was okay, then persuaded a couple of our players to help me up. It wasn't easy for him but I heard him say that if they offered their assistance, he would make sure I went off and hence not be in their way anymore.

Everybody knew something was seriously wrong because they were all telling me: "Stamp your foot, stamp your foot!" I did and promptly broke the standing-start world high-jump record.

John Bond, who was manager at the time, tapped Peter on the head with his Havana cigar and told him: "The sub's already on. Put Harry on the wing where he can do least damage." For the next 25 minutes, the lads passed to me more than they had throughout the previous 75 (sorry, but maths never was my strong subject) and I was delighted to hear the final whistle blow on our 1-0 defeat.

I hobbled into the medical room, which unfortunately, was right next to the home dressing-room at St Andrew's. I say 'unfortunately' because, as if I didn't feel bad enough, I also had to put up with Bondy's rantings and ravings.

He was having a right go at our forwards for missing chances and yelled: "I could have scored from those chances with my eyes closed - and I'm 40 something." The lads apparently looked puzzled, so he corrected himself. "Okay, I could have scored from some of those chances with my eyes closed - and I'm 50 something." Funny how you seem to become a better player when you've finished playing!

You had more chance of getting Joan of Arc to a bonfire than persuading the lads to stick around and listen to one of Bondy's preach-ins on his past playing prowess. Apparently it was John Bond in a Bobby Moore mask that captained the successful England side in 1966. His playing memoirs brought a new meaning to the word 'great', they certainly used to 'grate' on our nerves.

Whilst I lay there listening somebody tapped me on the shoulder and I turned round, taking my ear-plugs out at the same time. It was the doctor, who, I could immediately tell, had been gargling his favourite mouth-wash again. Somebody had gone to him in the bar with the message: "There's some-one badly injured, but it's one of ours, so don't rush."

He examined my leg and I said: "No Doc, it's the right one." Five minutes later, he said: "It's broken. Take this note to the Parkway Hospital in Solihull and they will sort you out." Hard to believe, but I actually had to drive myself 12 miles to the hospital. The club gave me directions, depite which I found my way.

I limped in, still wearing my Blues kit, to be greeted with the request from the receptionist: "What do you want?" I replied: "A BMX bike and a haircut like Steve Bull's, what do you think I want? I've broken my leg." She continued: "Oh, did you do it at the fancy dress ball?" I could tell from the polo neck socks she was wearing that she had a sense of humour.

Eventually, a big orderly arrived with a wheelchair which he told me to get into. I tried to explain that I had heroically played on the wing for 25 minutes and then driven to the hos-pital, so I didn't really need a wheelchair. He simply gave me one of those looks which said that if I didn't need one now, I soon would if I disobeyed.

I duly sat in it and went off to see the doctor, who encased me in Plaster of Paris from the tip of my toe to my groin. That was to present me with a few everyday problems but, as this book will be read by royals, I will say no more.

I rang my wife to tell her I was immobilised and received the distressed, sympathetic reaction I expected: "Who's going to pick the curry up then on the way home?" As Alice didn't drive, my brother-in-law, Des, was the only person available to come and pick me up from the hospital. It was slow going on the way home to Coventry. Looking back, it would have been better if he'd had a car but beggars can't be choosers. And at least you feel like the King of the Road when you're perched high in a JCB.

As for Birmingham City, they worried themselves speechless. So speechless that I didn't hear from them for three weeks and, even then, the contact only came because I rang in to query my wages. It was a simple query really, where were they? Carol, the receptionist, sidestepped the question with obvious practice and said: "What a coincidence! John Bond was just about to phone you to see how you were." I thought 'Yes and I'll play for England one day.' Do they think I'm stupid? No, don't answer that. Like I've always said, if God wanted footballers to think, he wouldn't have invented centre-halves.

Bondy came to the phone. "Harry, how are you my son, me old china, cor luvaduck! Any old iron? Knees-up, Mother Brown." You know, the typical Brummie! It was the end of the season by this time and he told me to be in at St. Andrew's the following morning at 10am. "Your contract is up, so don't be late," he warned.

I was there at 9.30am. I hadn't meant to be but I'd painted some 'go faster' stripes on my crutches and I'd fair whizzed along. Bondy summoned me in at 11am. "Well, Harry, your contract is up, you've got a broken leg, you're getting on a bit and the club's finances aren't in a very healthy state. But that's enough of the good news.

"You're going to have to take a drop in wages. Not much, just a bit to help the club through this difficult period. Mr. Wheldon (the chairman) and I have decided to cut your wages by 25 per cent. You have two choices: Either accept and be

Gordon Milne congratulates the winner of the break Harry's leg competition

grateful or decline and go on the dole. But, remember, you have got a broken leg."

I said: "If I accept a 25 per cent wage cut, I'll end up owing you."

It may not sound very fair, but Birmingham City called it business. I accepted. My leg may have been broken but my heart certainly wasn't when John Bond had the sack. In fact, it was one of the best parties I've ever been to. Fortunately, I made a full recovery and, even more fortunately, Garry Pendrey was appointed as the next manager.

8. Enjoying Blues

Things were totally different with Garry Pendrey and, in training, I started doing something I hadn't done for ages - enjoying myself.

I was presented with the Birmingham City Supporters' Player of the Year award watched by all the people who voted for me

As soon as you stop enjoying training, it becomes very hard work - and not too many of us like that!

Every morning, whether it was raining, snowing or just freezing cold, we would turn up and Gaz would be there, laughing, joking, cajoling and generally geeing us up. We used to swear he must be on happy pills but, no, it's just that he simply loves the game and seems to savour every minute he spends in it, The thing was: It was infectious. No, not Garry, his enthusiasm.

At Elmdon, Birmingham's training ground, they had the habit of forgetting to light the candle that heated the water up for the showers. That meant we used to cop the equivalent of an ice bucket when we came to get ourselves cleaned off when the morning's work was done. We used to rant and rave until the air, like our bodies, was blue but Gaz always showed us the way by jumping in first and giving us a song.

Mind you, he did have an advantage. He has such a hairy body that if he ever decided to become a streaker, he would have the anti-fur lobby, as well as the police, chasing him. I used to say to him: "You scratch my back, Garry, and I'll comb yours."

Garry's partner-in-crime at St. Andrew's was Tony Brown. I say partner-in-crime because some of the things they had us doing were criminal. 'Bomber' is a great lad but it was difficult to believe he had been such a prolific scorer of goals in his hey-day - most of them, it used to appear, against Coventry, where he seemed to score at will. Looking back, I don't think Will should have played. It was a great shame to see 'Bomber' shuffling around in practice games, barely able to run. He had a bad hip which required pain-killing tablets but he always had a smile in reserve. And that's where I saw most of him - in the reserves.

Garry Pendrey's football philosophy is simple: work hard and enjoy it. He always told us to enjoy the good times because bad times were likely to follow sooner or later. But why was he always looking at me when he said it? I remember once when we had whipped the wotsits off Villa at Villa Park

A meeting of the membership of my fan club

(please refer to the Unusual Moments in Sporting History book to verify this result) and Garry announced: "I'm off to the St. John's Hotel for a drink. I'm paying, everyone is welcome."

He didn't have to ask me twice. I was there, so was Steve Wigley, both of us Mancunians. I wonder if that's pure coincidence or just good upbringing. I couldn't believe it but none of the Scots lads turned up and they were the ones we said were mean! In fact, I think copper-wire was invented by Des Bremner and Andy Kennedy fighting over a penny.

Seriously, didn't the lads realise this was a great occasion? We had beaten the old enemy. Too many wanted to play the game and go straight home. They didn't realise that team spirit grew out of togetherness at times such as this. Don't get me wrong, I'm not advocating that footballers should live in each others' pockets but I do think they should celebrate or commiserate together after a game for a while.

During my happiest years at Coventry, win, lose or draw, we would meet at some designated pub, have a drink of lager, coke or even herbal tea, and discuss the events of the most important 90 minutes of our working week. I often ended up sitting next to Gary Gillespie, who, in the interests of uplifting my morale, would say something like: "I thought you did well today, Harry."

And I thought: right, if we're going to lie about it, you were magic, too. Only, when it was Gary, it wasn't normally a lie.

This mutual back-slapping would go on for about half-an-hour, by which time our egos were massaged and topped-up for another week. Then we would talk about what REALLY happened in the match. Another half-an-hour or so on and we would go home to pick up our wives and girlfriends (or both!) before meeting somewhere else for more of a social chit-chat.

Recently, I was talking to Stuart Pearce of Forest, we were comparing caps, at least I've got a better dentist than him! At Forest they still enjoy an after-match get-together and Gary Gillespie told me it was a regular Saturday evening ritual when he was at Liverpool. Mind you they've usually got three points to celebrate. Liverpool think 'DEFEAT' is where John

Barnes likes the ball played to.

Sadly, at Blues, the dressing-room, and the players' car park, an hour after the final whistle were like the Wimbledon terraces on a matchday. Empty. By and large, we wouldn't see each other again until Monday morning.

Considering Garry Pendrey had been a full-back all his playing life, he is quite a thinker. He used to say: "Life's too short to worry about bad games. Learn something from them but don't let them get you down. Just give me your best, I can't ask any more."

Another of his philosophies surfaced when a certain player got on our nerves by going on about how he had nearly scored in a game against Wolves. Before the next match, Gaz wrote on the dressing-room blackboard these words of wisdom: "Nearly is not good enough, never has been, never will be. Because nearly gets you nothing. Always has done, always will do." Now that's pretty profound for an ex-defender and he swore he never got it off the back of a matchbox.

If Garry was guilty of anything as Blues' manager, it was spreading himself too thinly (you wouldn't think that possible looking at him squeezed into his Wolves coach's tracksuit now). In other words, he probably tried to please too many people - the chairman, the board, the players, the tea-lady and anyone else he encountered along the way. He wasn't ruthless enough to say: "Sod you all, I'm doing it my way."

Garry was appointed as manager of the club he loved, to try to halt a slide. But it was like trying to halt a runaway train with the brake-block off a bicycle. His hands were tied in the transfer market and corners had been cut to such an extent that the very fabric of the club had been taken away.

It needed only a couple of injuries or a suspension (Robert Hopkins, come on down) and he had to try all manner of gambles. Mind you, I'm not knocking the sorry state of affairs completely. It was during such a pile-up of problems, coupled with a livewire forward called Tommy Wright, that I was given the chance to play centre-half for Blues - an experience I thoroughly enjoyed.

Being used as a sub again

I had been named yet again as sub for a game at Oldham and was busy removing the splinters from my backside as Tommy led our defenders a Wright dance, if they'll pardon me the pun. It's a bit worrying when you're named sub so often that they get you your own name plaque for the dug-out, all neatly carved out on the same sort of mahogany as is used for the chairman's car-parking space.

The worst thing about being sub, is having to sit next to the manager or coach. Gaz could shout for England. They used to have to postpone children's birthday parties in the houses opposite the dug-out on match-days. Garry would keep blowing the candles out on the cake.

Anyway, we were getting done on the Boundary Park plastic and he turned to me and said: "Can you play centre-half?" Modest as ever, I replied: "Can the Pope recite Latin?" My only concern was my height, or lack of it. On team photographs, I'd always had to either sit at the front or stand on a bench at the back.

But, if he was prepared to throw me in, I was prepared to give it a go, all 5ft 8in of me. Two minutes later, I was on. Three minutes later, I had been welcomed to the centre-halves' union with an elbow across the nose. Poor lad, his arm was almost broken. As chance would have it, I completely bottled little Tommy Wright up and I found Garry at the end of the game to ask him if he knew where Tommy was. When he said no, I pointed cheekily to my top pocket and said: "He's in here, Gaz!"

I was retained at centre-half for the rest of the season and probably played the best football of my career. Or the nearest I ever got to football. Actually, you don't need to play football at centre-half. Just ask Jim Holton, George Curtis, Vince Overson and, if he'll forgive me, Graham Turner. Your job is simply about good timing (I've never been late for a match yet) and stopping or intimidating the opposition. It's the only position you can fill and be cheered for consistently booting the ball into row G of the main stand.

It was amazing how the crowd took to me with their cheers.

It had previously been with their hob-nail boots. They were short of heroes at this time, so they took to chanting my name before kick-off. They knew it embarrassed me in front of the other players but they sang all the louder until I finally acknowledged them with a sneaky wave when none of my team-mates were looking. They even struck up a 'Harry for England' chorus, which was going a little too far. They must have known I was promised to the Iraq national side by then.

It was a very different picture to when I first moved to St. Andrew's around '84. That's the year '84, not at the age of 84. They used to jeer me at every opportunity then, even during the reading-out of the teams. At one stage, I grew to believe my name was Brian Robertsboo. It got that bad.

Although we were relegated under Garry Pendrey, I enjoyed my football with him as much as at any time. It was a sad day for me when he left. At that stage, I never dreamed that we would team up again at Wolves.

9. Managers

Now I am too old and wrinkly to be asked if I am 'that hunk out of the movies' or 'that heart-throb from the music-world,' the question that is thrown at me more than any other is: "Are you going to be a manager when you stop play-ing?" I usually reply: "No, I only have the one face." They laugh but I am being serious. To be a good manager, you have to be two-faced or even multi-faced.

For a start, you need one face for the players, another for the Press and another for your chairman and board. You cannot possibly act the same with all the interested parties in this high-profile game.

I know some managers who have had more faces than Big Ben and been successful. Unpopularity does not worry them. It would worry me senseless, though. If I did not mind being disliked, I would have been a policeman, a politician, a Poll Tax collector, Doug Ellis, the man who shouts 'Last Orders' in the pub, or the wife, or Gary Newbon. But I do dislike being disliked, if you see what I mean. I like people to like me and to say: "Look, there's Harry Roberts, I like him."

Anyway, I like all the managers I have worked with. Well, nearly all of them. Oops, it looks like I am developing a second face already.

Let me start with Dave Sexton, the nicest man I know. Honest. I know of no-one who has ever said a bad word against him. There are not many you can say that about. He has a deep knowledge of the game and enjoys a laugh in a dry sort of way. Trouble was, to the media, he used to come over as a dour sort of individual.

His training methods at Coventry were very technical and there were one or two lads who struggled to take everything in. Dave would tell us what a simple game football was and then spend the next half an hour baffling us with why it was so simple. It was more confusing than Father's Day at a referee's convention.

He was like a father figure to the lads at Highfield Road and protected us from the outside pressures that could have affected our football. But he was very much an anti-media man, which probably cost him his job at Manchester United at a time when John Bond was ruling the roost over the road at Manchester City.

Dave always managed to put us at ease. Before one game at Anfield, he sensed we were a bit uptight and, ten minutes before kick-off, thought it was time for a laugh. "What's that Ugandan fellow's name?" he said. "Idi Amin, wasn't it, boss?"

someone replied, to which Dave followed up with: "And how did he spell his first name?" "I-D-I," shouted Gary Gillespie - and, quick as a flash, Dave rounded off his party piece by saying: "Ho-de-ho!" The dressing-room erupted and the light-heartedness of it all did us the world of good. We only lost 4-0.

Dave's humour was so dry that we never knew if he was joking. Shortly after he joined the club, we were having crossing and shooting practice in training and Steve Hunt put over this lovely centre which I hoofed into a scrapyard about a quarter of a mile away. It surprised none of my colleagues that I missed the target. They knew I couldn't score in a brothel with a fiver sticking out of my ear.

But Dave was less understanding. He came over to me and said: "Zen Buddhism." I replied: "Harry Roberts, pleased to meet you, Zen." He said: "No. Think Zen Buddhism. Think the ball off you foot and into the net. You have heard of Zen Buddhism, haven't you?" Not wishing to sound ignorant of such everyday matters, I assured him I had heard of this person or creed or persuasion, but could he please give me a quick refresher course?

With that, the training session was halted and Dave told us to form a big circle and hold hands. It was like a scene from the primary school playground but, instead of singing ring-a-ring-a-roses, we were instructed to close our eyes and chant 'Zen, Zen, Zen' and 'feel the power in our bodies.' I chanted a couple of times and then slyly opened one eye to make sure I wasn't the only one indulging in this strange ritual. Out of the corner of my eye, I could see the boss on his back with his feet in the air, laughing his socks off. We couldn't believe we had been taken in. And my shooting still didn't improve.

Bobby Gould took over at Highfield Road in succession to Dave Sexton, just as we were going on a tour of Zimbabwe. One of his first decisions was to make me captain. Come the end of the summer break, my first match as skipper was in a 2-2 draw against Benfica in Lisbon. My second was for a 2-1 defeat at Scarborough in another friendly, from the sublime to the ridiculous, you might say.

Gouldy was a whole-hearted manager who expected the same dedication from his players. He was from Coventry and had played for the club more than a decade earlier, so there was Sky Blue blood running though his veins. He generated a lot of interest by going round workingmen's clubs and the like 'preaching the gospel' and he was an excellent P.R. man. When he made mistakes - and one was to publicly say Raddy Avramovic would never play in goal for the club again after letting a soft goal in - he learned from them and made sure they were not repeated.

He had never been a great player. Some might be unkind and say his second touch was usually a tackle. But he was very bubbly as a manager, a bit like Garry Pendrey. A great believer as well in his own ability, even if others doubted it. During his early days as an Albion player, he apparently won a cross-country race and laid into his new team-mates, telling them how slow they were by saying he usually came last in races at his previous club, Arsenal. The insult did not go down too well and one of the gathering replied: "Gouldy, if you ever make a manager, I'll bare my arse in Rackhams." As I say, he learned from his mistakes.

People at Coventry were rarely taken by surprise. They were used to innovative ideas from Jimmy Hill's days, but we players certainly had our eyebrows raised, a major task in my case, during one of Bobby's sessions. He sent us out for a five-a-side and, just before kick-off, told us there was to be no ball! Or, at least, only an imaginary one. It might have been a great idea for the Spot The Ball contest organisers but we found it all a bit tricky to handle. I think the score was still 0-0 (surprise, surprise) when Charlie George (nicknamed Kit-Kat because he'd been left with only four fingers following a lawnmower accident) walked off the pitch after receiving a short 'pass.' "Where the hell are you going?" thundered Gouldy. To which Charlie laughed: "Sorry, boss, I'm just going to get the ball. I let it roll under my foot for a throw-in!"

Gouldy never had that aura that some managers have. I never reached the point where I was hanging on his every

Dave Sexton confusing the squad with the introduction of tactics

word. But I do think he is a good manager with the ability to sign talented players from the lower divisions and then motivate them. He also earned our respect on the Zimbabwe trip when he breezed into a bar one night and ordered the young lads back to bed. We thought it went for us as well but, as we made our move, he said: "Right, what are you having to drink?" He stayed with us for a sing-song and we hit the pillow at about 2.30 in the morning. All part of the building-up-team-spirit process.

●   ●   ●   ●   ●

My abiding memory of Gordon Milne, another of my Coventry managers, is of his team-talks. They were something else, starting about two hours before kick-off and ending, amid drooping eye-lids and stifled yawns, an hour or so later. Asking Gordon to talk about the opposition was like asking Judith Chalmers to show you her holiday pictures.

His talks were interesting for about half an hour, then I would feel myself starting to doze off. I think it was all nervous tension - mine, not his. He could go on and on without repeating himself and would always finish with an adage or proverb adapted to his needs. Something like: "I can take you to the orchard, I can show you the apples on the trees, but it's up to you to reach up and grab one." I don't like apples and wondered what the hell he was on about. Then there was: "I can take you to the front door, I can unlock it, I can open it, but YOU have to walk through. I can't do that for you."

The fight to stay awake became a joke between Jim Blyth, our Scottish international goalkeeper and my best pal at Highfield Road, and me. We would look up at each other and start to giggle. I know it's childish but I was only 22 at the time. In the end, I didn't dare sit opposite Jim because he would deliberately make me laugh.

We were playing Manchester United one Saturday when Gordon, as usual, was delivering his speech. He came out with yet another saying, Jim's eyes met mine and he pulled a face. I

cracked up. Unfortunately, Gordon caught me trying to sup-
press my attack of the giggles and said: "Harry, what's so
funny?" I replied: "Nothing, it's just nerves". Gordon went on
angrily: "It's my little adages, isn't it?" and I was forced to own
up. I said: "It's near the end of the season, Gordon, and you've
come up with a different saying for 40-odd matches. How do
you do it?"

Gordon was clearly irritated and continued: "Well, funnily
enough, I've run out now, so you can think of one for next
week." I spent the next few days racking my brains but could
think of nothing witty (that's not unusual I hear you say). In
desperation, I turned to Jim Blyth for assistance. In the true
tradition of team spirit and camaraderie, he told me it was my
problem. Saturday came and my mind was still a blank. I had
rung the Samaritans and even they had hung up on me. Then
it came to me in a flash and I was able to relax into my usual
state of near-sleep as Gordon went into chapter and verse.

Every aspect of the opposition had been analysed and scru-
tinised, we had been told to do this and that, to do what we
had done the previous week and to have belief. At a minute to
two, I started to think I was going to get away with it. But, out
of the corner of his eye, Gordon caught me checking my watch
and said: "Oh, yes, that reminds me. Harry has got something
to tell us. A little gem to take out on to the pitch and help us
get two points" (I told you it was a long time ago). I felt 11
pairs of eyes pointing at me, none more interested than those
of Jim Blyth, who thought it was one big joke.

"You can take a horse to water," I offered "but a pencil
must be lead." The lads fell about laughing and Gordon managed a chuckle as he said: "It's not bloody easy, is it?" From
that day to this, I've never giggled again in a team meeting.
And I do appreciate how difficult it must be to talk non-stop for
an hour. After all, Gordon and my wife are the only people I
know who can do it.

Gordon, who was the only manager I've had who insisted
on being called by his christian name and not referred to as
'boss' or 'gaffer', was just the same when it came to contracts.

Spot the ball

You would decide in advance how much you were worth, then go into his office with your argument worked out and your speech rehearsed a dozen times over. The mood of grim determination was: "I don't care what Gordon says, I'm not budging. I won't accept a penny less." The reality was somewhat different.

You would walk in, sit down (I was not at the crawling or kneeling stage yet) and just be ready to deliver your ultimatum when he would say: "Did you see that programme last night? Oh, do you know anything about plants? Is this the right time of the year to put hyacinths in? It's just that my wife . . . you know Edith, don't you . . . of course you do, you met her at the Annual Soccer Ball . . .she was sitting next to the guest of honour, Eric Morecambe . . . we know him because he was born quite close to where we were born . . . Ernie, on the other hand, is from somewhere completely different . . . he's from Bolton . . . anyway this programme last night was all about Bolton." And so he would continue, leaving you with a headache and no idea whatsoever why you had gone in to see him in the first place.

Gordon's football knowledge was good, his man-management first-class and his day-to-day running of the club just as impressive. But what he really excelled in was the financial side of the game. He would have made a brilliant accountant. The club were always in the black, which is more than I can say about myself. My bank account has always been like a copy of Penthouse magazine left on the team-coach . . . well re(a)d!

Coventry were always renowned for grooming players and selling them for big money. Mick Ferguson (Everton), Dennis Mortimer (Aston Villa), Ian Wallace (Nottingham Forest), Garry Thompson (Aston Villa), Gary Gillespie (Liverpool), Harry Roberts (Birmingham City). Well, every £10,000 helps!

I think they built the Sky Blues Connexion, Coventry's training ground, with the money from Ian Wallace's sale. From mine, they brought the fertiliser for the pitches. I think there's a joke in there somewhere! Mind you, I was always telling our groundsman to put whisky into the sprinklers instead of water, so the grass would have grown half-cut.

Gordon always managed to keep us in the First Division, which was no mean feat, and he showed us the world. Boy, did he love an overseas trip. We were always popping off here and there.

The only place I didn't like was Saudi Arabia. Jimmy Hill had been made soccer supremo or something similar in the Middle East and was no doubt making plenty of sheckles for the privilege. What we got was a trip to the desert every couple of months to play matches against some Arab eleven or other. Those who have been there will probably know what I mean when I say it was a bitch of a place. It wasn't just hot, it was scalding. We couldn't sun-bathe because we would have been flambéed in 15 minutes. It seemed to be dusty and breezy all the time and we got sand blown into every bodily crevice I can mention, plus one or two I can't.

There was no booze, not that that bothered us as professional athletes (there goes my nose again) and we never saw a woman. They were all hidden behind those handkerchiefs. It was a real fun time, the sort of place which made a trip to the E.L.S. Bank Holiday sale seem like a riveting day-out. The locals would look at us as if to say 'How would you like your throat slit?' It was that bad I couldn't wait to see Coventry again.

The one redeeming factor for me was the price of gold on the outdoor markets. It was dirt-cheap. Every stall was dripping with the stuff. It was a bit like Ron Atkinson's dressing table, minus the hairspray. There was no pretence with appearances - the items were simply stuffed into every square inch of space and sold by the ounce, regardless of the product. I didn't mess about. I moved straight in for a fiver's worth of stud ear-ring for my mother-in-law's nose. It was high-quality stuff (the earring, not her nose).

It's a shame really because she was a bit hard of hearing and, apparently, when God was handing out noses, she thought he said 'roses' and asked for a big red one. She was

Never short of bottle at Blues

pleased that I had thought of her, bless her, but my purchases were nothing compared to Danny Thomas's. He used to buy so many chains for hanging round his neck that he arrived home looking like B.A. Barracus out of the A Team.

● ● ● ● ●

Continuing through the list of managers who've had the priviledge of working with me. What about Ron Saunders? Probably the shrewdest man I know. Well, he bought me, didn't he! His football outlook was very simple. Get the ball into their goalmouth and force them into mistakes. I felt sorry for the creative midfield players we had. If you had two touches in midfield, it was considered one too many.

The likes of Byron Stevenson, a Welsh international (big deal), had skill in abundance but just could not express themselves. I remember Byron saying once: "I've had enough of this." He decided to rebel and play a bit, but he lasted only 25 minutes before being hauled off. It would have been sooner but the substitutes' number cards had been mislaid! RS was going blue in the face calling him off but Byron ignored him until his number, quite literally, was up. Suffice to say he was not heard of a great deal at St. Andrew's after that.

When I joined Blues, Ron introduced me to all the lads as the new signing from Coventry. With the ink still drying on the signing-on documents, Ron went into this spiel about a telephone call he had just had that morning. "It was Bobby Gould," he said. "He didn't say anything, he just kept laughing." I felt terrible at this inference that Coventry had been delighted to see the back of me. But I need not have worried. This was a ritual. Something he did with all new boys to make sure they didn't get ideas above their station.

During one meeting, in order to gee us up, he told us to really get stuck in. To show absolute 100 per cent effort and determination. "Just imagine that the opposition are raping your wives or girlfriends, what would you do?" he asked. Andy Kennedy, none-too-keen on the physical side of the game, replied under his breath in his typical playboy style: "Take photographs." He was another who didn't play for a while.

My biggest fear with RS, though, was getting stuck in the sauna with him. No, not because of what you are thinking. It's just that he would have this uncanny knack of striking up a conversation just as you were getting out. The chat would invariably contain references to him being a corporal in the army and I used to think to myself: "So was Hitler." If you were trapped, you could normally write off the next half an hour. More than once I emerged like the turkey on Christmas morning, about two stones lighter and with a face like the Ribena Man.

But at least you always knew where you stood with Ron - or knelt if you were negotiating a new contract. He was never one to mince his words. If you were not doing the business, he would tell you in no uncertain terms. Something like: "My granny could do better than you and she's 78. Pull your finger out or I'll get someone else in who will."

He seemed to run the club from top to bottom. Chairman to tea lady. But, for all his hard exterior, he was lenient with some of the antics the lads got up to off the pitch. We had, at various times, Noel Blake, Mick Harford, Tony Coton, Robert Hopkins, Howard Gayle, Pat Van Den Hauwe and Billy Wright. They were just like the Magnificent Seven. They were more likely to turn up on Crimewatch than Saint & Greavsie.

● ● ● ● ●

John Bond. What can I say about him that won't get me into trouble? He made my life a misery at Birmingham. He used to turn up with his designer clothes and his big cigar. It isn't right that a man in his 50's should look better than me in a bomber jacket.

It always seemed to be: "When I was at West Ham, Bonzo and Mooro were this and that." He sounded like Alf Bloody Garnett! His training methods were brilliant, but only if you were a forward. I can say categorically (I can say it but I am not sure I can spell it) that in the year or so he was there, we did not do a single day's work on defending. You Blues fans probably noticed! His ideas on attacking play were fantastic and lads like Wayne Clarke and Robert Hopkins played the best football of their lives. He would say things like: "Hoppy, my son, I'll get you playing for England." And, if Bondy had stayed, he probably would have done. Trouble is we defenders would have been playing for the Rose and Crown.

Bondy was not the most mobile of blokes on the training ground. I soon came to the conclusion in five-a-sides that if I didn't pick out the third toe of his right foot with my passes to him, he would let the ball go by him. He and I had many an argument. He would call me useless and tell me to appreciate the game. I would call him a big fairy, and he nearly heard me once.

Birmingham City, quite simply, were not the right club for him. They were too unfashionable and they were run-down. How he would have loved one of those swish London clubs where he could have maintained the high profile he enjoyed. It's interesting that he had his best job (at Manchester City) at a time when the altogether more introvert Dave Sexton was just over the road at Manchester United.

Dave's departure was partly because he did not have the right image for the job. You could never say Bondy did not have the personality for the big appointment. At times, he acted the hard man and, at others, I thought he had a soft centre. He was not afraid to let his feelings be known, though, and he used to remind me of Roy Hattersley when he became angry. Without wishing to sound too coarse, I mean his saliva glands used to be on overtime. He's the only bloke I know with windscreen wipers on the inside of his car. I sat opposite him at a dinner once when he was in one of those slobbering moods. It took me three-quarters of an hour to finish my soup.

Not many people seemed to take a lot of notice of what John Bond had to say anyway. He once pulled Nicky Platnauer to one side in training and laid into him, storming: "Unfortu-

Back to training under corporal Saunders

nately, Him up there (God) did not give you any ability. My advice would be to quit and get a proper job." Nicky always seemed a bit nervous of the manager but can hold his head up high. He has made a good living from the game at a good many clubs and over quite a few years. And wasn't it Bondy who released Dean Saunders and Lee Dixon on free transfers?

Overall, I suppose I would best sum up the required qualities of a football manager by saying he needs to be both introvert and extrovert; Catholic and Protestant; black and white; arrogant and humble. I wonder what Derek Hatton is doing next season?

10. The Players Do

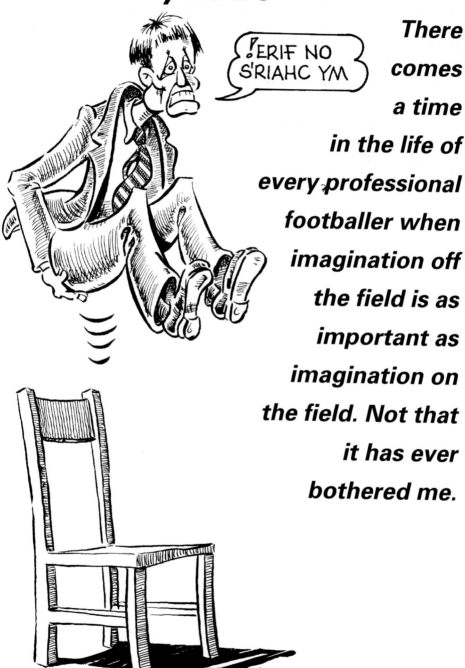

There comes a time in the life of every professional footballer when imagination off the field is as important as imagination on the field. Not that it has ever bothered me.

Christmas for the normal working man or woman is celebrated on December 25 (December 1 to January 5 if you happen to be in middle or senior management). For footballers, though, Christmas usually falls on a day early in December. Let me explain.

To us, the festive season means abstinence, fast and a glut of matches aimed at getting supporters away from their TVs and turkeys. OUR turkeys meet their maker around the first week of the month in an unannounced 'fixture' we call 'the players' do'. This is OUR celebration, usually staged on a Tuesday or Wednesday afternoon, when tracksuits are swopped for party hats, streamers and funny big noses. I just go as I am.

Once there, we partake of a dry sherry or twelve and start to discover how well we've overcome one of our annual headaches: what to do for entertainment? A video of Robert Hopkins' last fight, perhaps? No, that was a first-round knock-out. Or a Dave Mackay tactics video? Unfortunately, we couldn't find one. Last Christmas, a film of Brian Clough kissing TV presenters was suggested but we all fancied a change.

It's certainly a problem because we footballers are mollycoddled to such an extent that everything is normally done for us. We don't usually have to think for ourselves until we get out on the field. Christmas party decisions tend to be taken in September. That's when we have a players' meeting to elect the person most suitable to organise the day's fun and frivolity.

It has to be someone who has sufficient gift of the gab to convince all those in a drunken stupor that they're having a great time. And it has to be a big enough divvy to be prepared to take the blame if the whole thing flops. You've guessed it! I'm now in my 12th year as chief organiser of the players' do.

In doing the spadework, you have to take into account that the average footballer (and I know plenty of average footballers) is a p...-taker extraordinaire, is never satisfied, is only here for the beer and could always have done better himself with his eyes closed.

You must also remember that, when it comes to Christmas

entertainment, the seasoned pro has seen it, done it, read the book, bought the T-shirt, told every joke the comedian tells and won numerous Oscars as No. 1 heckler of sub-standard acts.

One such person springs readily to mind – a great laugh and a great bloke, but not the easiest audience member as far as a stand-up comic is concerned. At the time, player X was going bald at an embarrassing rate. If loss of hair starts off as a B road, he was in the six-lane motorway stage. Only the week before, in fact, he had been to see the club doctor to see if he knew anything to keep his hair in. Much to his dismay, he was handed a cardboard box.

The player, having had an odd few drinks, as well as a few normal ones, decided the comedian's jokes were older than Peter Withe's suits and started to show his displeasure. Now, if you ask me, there are a few golden rules to follow in life: never threaten anyone bigger than you, never threaten anyone faster than you, definitely never threaten anyone who is both bigger and faster than you (everyone in my case), never tie your shoe-laces in front of Justin Fashanu and never ever heckle a comedian who has a microphone.

On this occasion, the player in question broke that last rule continuously and then looked around for support from his team-mates, who were cowering away from the onslaught we knew would follow. He was subjected to one of the best put-down lines I've ever heard. Remember that it was directed to a man whose hair was fast waving him goodbye. Face-to-face with the comic, the player giggled, a helpless lamb to the slaughter. "Do you play golf?" enquired the comedian. "Of course I do," came the reply. Then, patting the player's bald head, he added: "Then you should know – you should replace ALL divots." The heckling ceased and the player retired to the bar to lick his wounds. Which reminds me: Jim Blyth has got a lovely pub just outside Birmingham if you fancy a good pint!

As far as I'm concerned, the players' do to beat all players' dos was the Coventry knees-up we had in 1983 at the Stocks nightclub just outside town. Muggins was in charge once again and, to be daringly different, had opted to book a hypnotist called Johnny Hilliard. The lunch started at midday and, no sooner had I started my soup, than I got called away to the phone. It was the hypnotist. He was lost and asked me the best way to the club. I said: "Let me think . . ." He replied: "Thanks very much" and put the phone down. I thought: 'Bloody hell, he's good.'

I was in the company of a friend from Manchester, Bob Harrison, a very busy businessman, so busy he had travelled down the night before so he wasn't late. He warned me against hiring the hypnotist for obvious reasons, however we decided if we dispensed the beer, wine and liquers in sufficient quantities and frequency, that most of the lads would be completely relaxed and that much easier to control. The lads were of great help in this direction and we received no problems in achieving our aim. In fact, they made liquid relaxation an artform.

They went under the influence, all right. Unfortunately, it was an alcoholic one, rather than the hypnotist's.

As entertainment time approached, the lads were seated in rows of six in front of the stage. Looking at some of the faces, we were confident the hypnotist, who had arrived by this time, had been given a head start, courtesy of the Carlsberg, Chablis and Remy Martin.

Gary Gillespie, Trevor Peake, Micky Adams, Nicky Platnauer, Steve Hunt and Garry Thompson were among the players present and, in quiet, soothing tones not unlike those of John Sillett, we were told to join our hands together and slip into a deep, deep sleep. Nicky Platnauer thought it was 3pm on a Saturday afternoon!

"You are totally relaxed," the hypnotist said. "Your eyes are heavy. When I click my fingers, you will be awake but you won't be able to unlock your fingers from your entwined hands." When the signal came, most opened their eyes, released their hands and laughed. A few, however, couldn't, including Bob Harrison, who had been the biggest sceptic of the lot a few minutes earlier.

The hypnotist was first-class. In no time at all, he had Steve Hunt leaping six feet out of a chair he thought was on fire (Steve could never do that for England, let alone Coventry) and believing he was from Mars. The two of them spoke Martian to each other and the rest of us looked mystified at all this gobbledygook. It was a bit like listening to a conversation between Bully and Andy Thompson, the two Black Country lads, at Wolves.

Next came my mate Bob, who suddenly jumped up and started tap-dancing to the tune 'Lullaby of Broadway'. Mickey Adams, who thought all this was hilarious, was next in the humiliation stakes. First, he unhesitatingly ate a lemon he was told was the world's most succulent peach, then he was handed a pair of cardboard 'X-ray' glasses which supposedly gave him the power to see through female clothing.

A barmaid, who had earlier been boasting no man could ever get her under his power, then did her induced party-piece - a belly dance that nearly made us sick. No man could ever control her, she said. Nor could any corset. She was so ugly that peeping Toms used to knock on her windows and ask her to draw the curtains.

Virtually at a click of his fingers, the hypnotist could snap the exhibitionists out of their hilarious acts and restore them to normal behaviour, totally unaware of what they had been doing. Then snap, they were 'performing' once more, finally lining up for a striptease which, fortunately, ended at the underwear stage. Fortunately, because I've seen the players completely undressed and it's not a pretty sight.

This story will confirm the suspicions of supporters who think many of their team's players are in a different world on Saturday afternoons. Maybe they really are! And what about hypnosis as a form of motivation? Perhaps that might explain how Peter Beardsley won a modelling contract and how Lenny Henry found inspiration in developing his black Spiv character Delbert Wilkins around Dave Bennett (the ex-Man City and Coventry winger), the only difference being deep down Delbert is a likeable character. And, even more unbelievably, how

David Icke was persuaded not only to claim he was the Son of God, but, more improbable still, to wear a turquoise tracksuit.

Anyway, Johnny Hilliard made such an impact at Coventry that, flushed with success, I subsequently booked him to entertain my team-mates at Blues when I had moved on a year or two later. What a disaster that turned out to be!

For months before Christmas, I was extolling his virtues and telling the lads what a tremendous do they were in for. You didn't like to disappoint or annoy the likes of Noel Blake, Mick Harford, Tony Coton and Howard Gayle and I thought I couldn't go wrong.

I went through the same pre-trance routine of telling the lads it would be best if they were relaxed in case they were called on stage. They weren't so much relaxed as comatose when Johnny arrived and asked for volunteers. Gerry Daly and I, as organisers, were the only ones who would get up. Come to think of it, considering all the booze that had been consumed, I think we were the only ones who COULD get up.

Eventually we badgered a couple of others into joining us and Johnny went to work. He should have gone home. He couldn't hypnotise us to save his skin - and it quickly became obvious that's what he needed to do. Boy, did I try to go 'under'! I reasoned that if I was in a trance, I wouldn't feel the pain the St. Andrew's heavies were sure to dish out.

I even tried popping a Mogadon in my mouth, but I was still in the wide-awake club. After three-quarters of an hour (footballers are quick to catch on, you know) the lads realised things weren't going according to plan. On came the bread rolls, followed by the roast potatoes. Johnny Hilliard was obviously on a diet because he left the stage quickly and locked himself in his dressing-room.

Much to the disbelief of Jim Blyth, Gerry Daly had handed over the money before the act and Johnny couldn't understand the no-trance-no-cash line Jim was pursuing. Now, Jim Blyth is not a man to mess around with. I roomed with him for years on all Coventry's overnight trips and still have the scars to prove it. He's big, strong, Scottish and, what's more, he's a goalkeeper.

As Johnny Hilliard was scurrying towards his Jaguar, Jim politely asked for our money back - and was equally politely refused. Jim was quite adamant and grabbed hold of his victim and threw him into the car. As a farewell offering, he started to pour red wine over Johnny's shirt, suit and upholstery. That was ill-advised. Jim should have known you have white wine with chicken.

Talk about w(h)ine, you should have heard Johnny. He got his car started and shouted as he zoomed off: "You haven't heard the last of me." Jim was inviting him back to Birmingham with inducements like: "I'd like to put YOU under! About six feet under!" Johnny was true to his word, though, and it wasn't long before Ron Saunders was asking whether any of us knew anything about a hypnotist who didn't like wine (or at least didn't like it poured over the inside of his gleaming car). We said 'no' and that was the last we heard of the matter. Ron was good at smoothing over things like that. Mind you, he had had plenty of practice.

I think that was the day I made the decision never to organise another players' do.

11. Being Noticed

Things always happened when Steve Whitton and I were together. Occasionally, these 'things' involved unwanted females, as I will explain.

I know mine has never been the prettiest face God created - in fact, in a bonny baby contest once, I finished last behind a bulldog chewing a wasp. My mother told me I was so spotty and warty when I was a baby, that she came out of the shops one day and there was a blind man reading my face. But the level of interest in me sometimes increased when I was with Steve.

While we were out together one night, we were being bothered by this girl who was no oil painting herself. If pigs could fly, she would have been a squadron leader. Put another way, even the Man from Del Monte would have said no. She kept trying to attract Whit's attention, though, so we had to put our well-rehearsed 'sob story' routine into operation.

I took her to one side and suggested she ask Steve how his sister's piano lessons were going. To give her due credit, she didn't come out with the question point-blank, but casually let it slip after sidling over to him some time later. As soon as she said it, Whit's face dropped and, amid pretend crying, he unleashed a torrent of anger at her. The girl's face was a picture. "What's wrong?" she said. "What have I said?"

Damned groupies!

92

Eventually, a 'tearful' Steve sobbed: "My sister's got no arms." To which she replied, pointing in my direction: "It . . . it . . . it was him over there." And she added to my face: "You're sick you are, you're a pervert."

I apologised to her and confessed I had done the same to him before and felt so guilty afterwards I had bought his sister a present - a watch. But that had been embarrassing as well, what with people asking her the time and seeing her lift up her leg to study her ankle. That really did it. The groupie stormed off, never to be seen again.

On another occasion, Whit and I were in 'The Wallace', a pub situated in the Keresley mining village just outside Coventry. It was only a stone's throw from the pit itself. You could tell that because all the windows were broken, but it kept the fires burning. This establishment was frequently visited by miners and rugby players. Worse still, some of the locals were rugby-playing miners.

It's a well-known fact that footballers and rugby players don't really hit it off together and it wasn't long before one rugby lad took offence to the fact that we were breathing. He wasn't shy about telling us so and Whit stuck his chin out and challenged our adversary to do something about it.

His chin was like a red rag to a bull. If actions speak louder than words, this guy was absolutely deafening. He whacked Whit so hard that he hit the floor like a sack of spuds. The lad then turned to me and I began to wish I had donned my training shoes. But fear is a strange thing and, closing my eyes, I swung a real hay-maker that landed on its target and left Giant Haystacks in a crumpled heap next to Steve.

Boy, I felt good and went over to tell Whit: "You can get up now, I've sorted him out." But he was still out cold and, worse still, the Man Mountain three Shredded Wheat-eater was not only up and about but also sobering up fast. I thought to myself: 'Well Harry, you've had a good innings mate, but this is it.' Yet I somehow found the courage and strength to pin him to the ground and hold him in a bear-hug until people stepped in to separate us. Once I knew we had both been properly restrained, I started shouting: "Let me at him, let him fight, I'll kill him!" Thank God they didn't. As for Steve Whitton, he might not have been much of a fighter but he throws a mean chin!

12. On Tour

What did Barry Powell get that Mick Ferguson was too slow to get?

No, not a coaching job at Wolves, but a prize souvenir from Coventry's trip to New York a decade or so ago.

Steve Hunt had just been bought from New York Cosmos and part of the deal was that we would fly out to the States to play a friendly and experience a slice of that magnificent American hospitality. Life can be a real bitch at times can't it?

New York – New York

As well as sampling those tremendous stadiums and being wined and dined by Warner Bros representatives on the 107th floor of the World Trade Centre (we would prefer to have eaten off tables, but the views of one of the world's most exciting cities were breathtaking) we found ourselves in quite the most splendid hotel I've ever stayed in. I've seen some rough ones, believe me. You know, the sort that steal YOUR towels, but this was a real beauty. It had everything - hot and cold running waiters, ex-directory room service and a sauna that was so formal you needed a collar and tie to get in.

The Cosmos were at the height of their popularity and the razzamatazz was incredible. Most of the 40,000 crowd munched picnics on the stadium concourse before the game (can't quite imagine that happening on the Asda car park outside Molineux!) and the players were 'introduced' to them by loudspeaker just before kick-off.

As the Cosmos stars ran out one by one, they slapped the hands of the beautiful cheer-leaders lined up at the entrance of the pitch. When it was our turn, I have never known so many people be dazzled by the sun. The girls were again slapped - but not too many of them on the hands. It must have been the only time in the short history of American soccer that the cheer-leaders slapped the players back in retaliation!

As we lined up for the official introductions, our manager Gordon Milne - a true English gent - was standing next to man-of-the-moment Steve Hunt. Gordon, one hand behind his back in military style, slacks with creases that could slice bacon and shoes so well polished he was distracting the planes hovering above the Big Apple, was just about to have his hand shaken when Steve's face was spotted by the approaching dignitary.

"Steve baby, how are you? Gimme five!" And, amid the sort of welcome normally reserved for a Harlem Globetrotter, Steve was surrounded by well-wishers, leaving Gordon looking as out of place as a pork sandwich at a barmitzvah.

The limelight wasn't Steve's exclusive property, though. We all did some mingling with the football VIPs later and that's where Baz Powell and Fergy come in. We had lost the match 3-1 (well, we let them win because they had just sold us Steve Hunt; the fact that they were three times better than us had nothing to do with it), but we were all determined to win the race for the big prizes at the shirt-swapping ceremony afterwards.

We all wanted a souvenir of the trip and there was some hectic exchanging and rushing about afterwards. Pelé and Franz Beckenbauer raced towards me pleadingly, almost ripping the material off my back, but I managed to shake them off and tell them to go and get someone else's shirt. All the Cosmos jerseys had a player's name on the back and I managed to get one that I hung proudly above the fireplace when I got home. Only problem is I couldn't remember there being anyone called C. Rap in their side.

Apart from me, Pelé, who presented us all with tankards

The only thing I got my leg over on tour!

afterwards, was the main attraction. He had made a point of telling me he wanted a word after the game and I could hardly wait for the final whistle. I never did double-check the meaning of what he said but I'm told it was Brazilian for: "If you ever kick me again, I will personally attach the most sensitive part of your anatomy to your ears." It was a moment I will treasure forever.

Baz, meanwhile, was so eager to get the shirt of Marinho that he ignored his opponent's polite refusals and followed him all the way to the dressing-rooms. He finally got his reward, as we all did, whether it was that worn by Pelé, Francisco Marinho, Formoso, Carlos Alberto or Beckenbauer.

All, that is, apart from Mick Ferguson. Mick was a bit slow off the mark (not for the first time eh, Mick?), so he asked Steve Hunt to use his contacts to get him one. Steve duly obliged and, to a wide-eyed and expectant Fergy, revealed the name on the back . . . TERRY GARBETT!!! He had taken one of the reserves' shirts as a joke and reduced us all to laughter.

But Fergy showed his sense of humour too. Next day, he made a bee-line for one of New York's top tailors and requested a small addition to the ridiculed garment. Unimpressed by the ordinariness of the name Terry Garbett, he had jazzed it up with a final 'O' that made it a more exotic Terry Garbetto!

On the trip, we were within striking distance of the chic Studio 54 nightclub frequented by the likes of Mick Jagger, David Bowie and Rod Stewart. Crowds turned up just to stand outside and watch the stars roll up but coach Ron Wylie had no truck with all this glitz. He had us over there to try to win and banned us from going in search of the bright lights. Shame really. It would have been quite something to turn up at my local in Coventry and kick off with the line: 'As I was saying to Rod in the doorway of Studio 54 . . .'

● ● ● ● ●

In spite of the razzamatazz of New York, one of the best club tours I've ever been on was with Birmingham to Majorca, that little-known Mediterranean isle of mystique on to which the lager louts descend every year in their thousands. The club paid for it (well, the bus fare to Elmdon Airport anyway) and made it voluntary. I was dead against going but my wife insisted I went - and you know what women are. They always get their way in the end.

Once in the resort, we paired off into rooms, the two really good-looking lads together (Steve Wigley and me), two single lads not quite so good looking (Steve Whitton and Andy Kennedy), the uglies (John Frain and Adrian Bird) and so on. Much to our disappointment, we were staying in an up-market area well away from Magaluf (our choice of venue), but the club had done us proud with the accommodation.

It was the only time we Blues lads had said we liked the villa - it was like something out of Knot's Landing. Complete with walled courtyards, orange groves, magnificent plants and flowers and expensive leather furniture. Very similar to home really (Steve Bull's home anyway). The kitchen, with every

Round to Bully's for lunch

labour-saving device imaginable, was like an advert for Zanus-si and they'd even left enough food for a week – if you happened to be Lester Piggott on a diet. From the lounge, expansive patio doors led to steps that cascaded down to the azure blue waters of the Mediterranean. You wouldn't think I was a footballer coming out with phraseology like that, would you? A binman yes, but not a footballer.

We'd been booked in for a week but I was homesick after a day. (Well, you never know, my wife might be reading this flannel.) As soon as we unpacked, we donned our cossies and headed for the beach. I'd just bought new swimming gear as my last set had a hole in the elbow and I felt a million pesetas as I stretched out horizontally on the sand.

The next bit of the story reads like a day-trip to the English seaside. The heavens opened the moment we splashed on the factor 15 and we decided it was time for liquid refreshment. Rain doesn't half make you thirsty, we all commented, and retired to the nearest hostelry for tea and biscuits.

There must have been something wrong with their Typhoo,

though, because it didn't half give me a headache. There's a tip for you: don't drink foreign tea - it gives you a hangover. I stuck to the lager after that and never had a problem.

It wasn't long before we received our marching orders from the bar. Now, Adrian Bird (what a name that is - didn't his parents like him?) is a clever lad, cleverer in fact than Bamber Gascoigne's cleverer brother if I can slip into a bit of Rowan Atkinsonese. He has brains coming out of his ears, so why he ever wanted to be a professional footballer I don't know. But the one thing he doesn't know about is holding his drink.

Half a Cherry B, topped off with a Snowball, and he had lost the use of his legs and the contents of his stomach. Unfortunately, he chose to do the latter over the manager of the bar, so it was a case of 'on yer bike' with something a little less pleasant than 'Adios Senors'. We carried Adrian back to the villa, still singing his head off. A sort of Birdy song, you might say. We knew his first words next morning would be 'never again'. And they were. He was true to his pledge, too, until that evening at least. But we still had to wean him back onto the hard stuff with Wine Gums and Ovaltine.

I, on the other hand, had problems of a different kind. We subsequently managed a bit of time in the sun - a commodity which, my friends will tell you, has the knack of turning a part of my anatomy a bleached white. I remember strutting contentedly along a near-deserted shore one day and feeling proud when a guy looked at me, then woke up his dozing wife. I was flattered to think I had been recognised - then flattened to realise he had in fact just been pointing out to her the colour of my infamous eyebrows. I gave him a dirty look, stuck my head in the air arrogantly and promptly tripped over a stone. What a prat!

From then on, I wore strategically-placed goggles, which brought a few funny looks in the discos and art galleries, I can tell you. But I know a few people who would be quite happy to have such eye-brows. Ron Atkinson, for instance, would be able to sweep them back over his head to make him appear to have a full head of hair.

Misfortune overtook me again, though, when a few of us indulged in a little catching practice with a floating ball in the sea. With my first throw, the ball wasn't the only thing that left my hand at a fair rate of knots. My wedding ring did likewise, which presented me with two immediate problems. First, my wife would go mad but, secondly and more seriously, the girls would think I was single and refuse to leave me alone.

The lads understood my twin anxieties and joined me in a search that would have done Jacques Cousteau proud. I even persuaded Scot Andy Kennedy to lend a hand by telling him it was a £1 coin we were looking for. I spent so much time on the sea-bed that I felt like the Man from Atlantis and noticed my feet starting to web. The search was called off in failure. But I did the next best thing and rushed to buy a curtain ring for my naked finger. The girls were already starting to flock around me and would have made the week hell.

● ● ● ● ●

If Majorca was a boozy trip, what about the jaunt I had with Coventry to the Far East in 1978? We had been invited to the prestigious Japan Cup competition, along with FC Cologne, Ajax and a crack Brazilian team whose name I am much too embarrassed to try to spell or pronounce.

It was an unforgettable experience, complete with a stop-over in Alaska, a journey on the Bullet train at well over 100 miles per hour and, most importantly, the chance to sample the strange but wonderful way of Japanese life.

We were away for 14 days, during which my wife was due to give birth to our first child. So, erring on the side of safety, I purchased six magnums of champagne at Heathrow Airport, ready at a moment's notice to play my part in the wonderful concept of childbirth - wetting the baby's head!

Don Nardiello, a Welsh-born lad of Italian parentage and thick Brummie accent, was my room-mate. He was just the sort Alice would have chosen for me. He never smoked, never drank and never sought the company of loose women. And he made all his own dresses! He was a good player, too. He would never have played for Wales otherwise, would he!!!!

The tournament was staged at two venues, Osaka and our base, Tokyo, with teams playing each other on a league basis. We were runners-up to Cologne in our group, which meant we had to travel to Osaka to play the Brazilians in the semi-final.

We travelled there by Bullet, a train capable of journeying at over 100 miles per hour at a time when Jimmy Saville and British Rail were getting there at only a fraction of the speed. It was an experience enjoyed by all of us and one BR could have learned a lot from, although, as a regular customer of theirs, I can tell you that they didn't!

Because we had all done well in the tournament, a sports company called Onitsuka Tiger, who later became known as Asics, asked Gordon Milne whether we would be interested in doing a TV advert endorsing their boots. The lads were none too keen, until they heard of the yen involved. Then we were all in the make-up room quicker than it used to take Joe Bugner to hit the canvas.

It wasn't the most demanding role in the history of the small screen. All we had to do was smile, hold up a boot and say 'Tiger'. But they had forgotten we were footballers - a species which could think things or do things, but not simultaneously.

The producers became a little irritated when some of the lads held up a tiger and said 'Boot' but, with the wonders of technology, we finally got the commercial in the can. We longed to see the finished article on TV and, back at the hotel, were told to report to rooms 1001 and 1002. I thought that a bit strange as it was only a 250-room hotel.

Eventually, we found them and, when we walked in, it was like an Aladdin's Cave or a Santa's Grotto, with boots, trainers and sportswear piled up almost to the ceiling. What's more we were told to help ourselves. Well, the Japanese aren't the biggest of races and three of our hosts were nearly killed in the crush.

It was like Gary Lineker's spare room but it emptied quicker

Overseas habitat - Coventry in Majorca

than my bank account when the wife gets hold of my cash card. I came away with enough gear to stock a small sports-shop. I still wear some of it now, especially this one shirt with Tiger emblazened across the front. I wear that in bed.

Anyway, after losing the semi-final in Osaka, we returned to our hotel in Tokyo. I'd been ringing home every day hoping to hear I'd become a father but Alice, as usual, wouldn't give up without a fight. It gradually became clear that I would be back in Coventry, rather than away in the Land of the Rising Sun, when the little one arrived.

This put me in a dilemma. Because of weight restrictions on the plane, I was unable to take home both the sports-gear and the champers, so it was decided by the lads — without any consultation with me, I might add — that there would be an end-of-tour party in the Roberts/Nardiello room. The boys were very helpful like that.

Donato Nardiello, the Cliff Richard of the football world,

I still wear the shirt

wasn't too pleased. His idea of a fun night out was a jam session on tambourine whilst gargling a pint of Lourdes water and simultaneously reciting the Old Testament down the local Sally Army hall. Poor Don, he couldn't convert a good cross to a goal, never mind a skinhead to Christianity. It was common practice for him to take a couple of Aspirin after eating a packet of Wine Gums.

We made it a 'bring a bottle' party but, where Don got a bottle of milk from at 9pm in Japan, I don't know! With a full compliment of players, though, and the champagne going down faster than John Bond's opinion of yours truly, the party was in full swing. All it needed to set it off completely was for Don to put down his milk and try a drop of bubbly, so I put a cunning scheme into operation.

I announced to the gathering that I was nipping out to phone home and see if there was any news. Five minutes later, I returned, a smile on my face and the words 'It's a boy! It's a boy' pouring joyously from my mouth. Everybody cheered and I said a few words to the effect: "Come on, everybody raise a glass of champagne to the new arrival — you as well Don."

Well, once Don had taken a sip, there was no stopping him. He cast aside all his inhibitions and well and truly got into the spirit of things. Half an hour later, he was anybody's, bumping into furniture, clattering into his team-mates, singing and generally making a nuisance of himself, much more natural behaviour for a footballer.

I showed him the red card and put him to bed, where he was asleep in a matter of seconds, oblivious to the drunken scenes around him and to the practical joke he had been the victim of. My first job next morning was to tell him that the noise the previous evening had drowned out the end of my announcement. What I had actually been trying to say was: "It's a buoy — that red thing in the lake next to the hotel. It's a buoy." Or at least that's what I told him.

Actually, it's just as well the baby wasn't born that night because we had wet his head so much, the poor thing would have come out needing a snorkel!

● ● ● ● ●

Then there was the time Coventry went to the Faroe Islands to play a match. I think ours was the biggest plane that had ever landed there. The airport staff didn't have any steps big enough, so we had to jump the last few feet to terra firma.

Not only did they not have proper steps, they didn't seem to have any booze on the island either. But we found some - loads of the stuff - when we were invited to a private party at a house. It was around this time that I decided drinking and driving was no good for you. As a result, I cut right down on my driving. Not that drinking ruled my life. My binges were restricted largely to hell-raising nights out with the mother-in-law because I didn't want to turn out like George Best - rich, famous, enormously gifted, surrounded by beautiful girls and unaware that I had been on the Wogan show until the following morning.

Back on the Faroes, we had to take our shoes off before we entered the house. I don't know whether it was the local custom or just a case of being house-proud. Anyway, we all obliged - and then filled our boots with the alcohol on offer.

We were all well gone by the time we departed and had terrible trouble finding the right shoes. We could see our hotel in the distance and, not fancying the walk down the windy country lane, decided to take a more direct route across the fields.

As a decision, it was about as successful as choosing King Herod as a babysitter. We crossed from one field to the next by jumping over a wall and found ourselves virtually up to our waists in mud. It was a bit like playing at Hartlepool on a wet Tuesday night in November.

The problem was that we still had our club suits on and were in an advanced state of filth by the time we reached the hotel. There was only one thing for it - we jumped into the showers fully clothed and at least made it look as though we had encountered nothing worse than an unfriendly downpour!

13. The Players

Hand on heart, I can honestly say I have always been completely professional in my out- look to foot- ball. To training, to early nights, to giving my clubs 100 per cent.

But it's important to me for fans to realise that not all play-ers are stars. Some of us have limited ability. We're rank-and-file players. And players of limited ability should not be pillo-ried if they give of their best.

Sometimes, no matter how hard you try, things don't go for you. And it seems the harder you try, the worse things become. It's then you really need the crowd to lift you, not to get on your back, because your head feels like a lead weight.

When I hang my boots up, I would like my football epitaph to read: "Harry Roberts: never a genius on the ball, but always guaranteed to give his all."

● ● ● ● ●

I have come up against all sorts of players in my career. The skillful, the not so skillful. The ordinary and the extraordinary footballers. One player in particular brings back some painful memories.

I can't believe I came so close to death after what seemed such a good idea at the time. We were playing mighty Leeds at Elland Road and had a back-four that resembled a Tom Thumb convention. There was Graham Oakey at right-back, Bobby McDonald at left-back, Mick Coop in the middle and yours truly at his side. Leeds had Joe Jordan leading their attack and Gordon McQueen lending his support at corners and free-kicks. Which was a tall order by any standards.

Now Joe was never the easiest player to play against. I think the usual football cliché to use at this point is: "You always knew you had been in a game when you had faced Joe Jordan." To say he was intimidating was as obvious a state-ment as saying my old Coventry skipper, George Curtis, was no Maradona.

Our manager, Gordon Milne, suggested it might not be a bad idea every now and then at corners to unsettle big Joe by accidentally stepping backwards on to his toes so he couldn't get airborne.

Due to his menacing reputation, I guarantee that you will

never again see a defender so keen to keep the ball from going for a corner. However, all was to no avail and Leeds duly won the first of many corners, Eddie Gray swung it in, I stepped backwards . . . and 'lost' the next few minutes of my life. When I woke up, I had a crowd around me and was seeing stars. Not just those in the Leeds line-up either. While I had 'accidentally' stepped on Joe's toes, his elbow had 'accidentally' come into contact with my head. I was out cold and came round to be greeted by the sight of Joe grinning that horrible toothless grin down at me. It's funny how, off the field, he could do a passable impression of a Colgate toothpaste rep. On the field, he was more like Dracula with muscles in his gums.

Anyway, he leaned down and helped me up (now that's what I call a gentleman) and said in those dulcet Scottish tones of his: "If you EVER do that again, son, I'll take your head completely off." I thanked him for his warning and for his assistance and suggested that, if he felt so inclined to repeat the treatment later in the afternoon, could he please put a splodge of Vic on his elbow as I had the start of a head cold. He wasn't amused. I tried making it up to him in the players' bar afterwards by offering him a drink. I went to buy a pint of lager, but Joe said he'd prefer aperitif!

Strangely enough, I actually had one of my best games that day and was later described by Terry, (or was it Tommy) Cooper as 'one of the best young defenders in the country.' It was just the towns and cities where I struggled. Because of the concussion, I didn't know the score and had to ask one of the lads as we walked off who had won. Gordon said it was a pity I couldn't be concussed every week if it meant I was going to play that well. I thought to myself that I did feel concussed most weeks - normally after one of Gordon's team-talks! In later years, I tried to revive that old Roberts magic by banging my head a few times against the dressing-room wall before we went out. It didn't do any good, I still didn't know the score and I got the legs run off me more often than not. But, in later years, I've realised I must have made an impression on my various managers. During matches, I've had them banging their heads against the roof of the dug-out!

● ● ● ● ●

Steve Bull is the type of player who has a great presence and aura on the field, but off the field he is a fairly quiet unassuming type of guy who even finds it embarrassing to sit in a hairdressers which is probably why he employs the council to cut his hair. He likes nothing better after a game than to go back home and enjoy a few pints in the local with his mates, he's so unassuming that he never fails to invite his chauffeur in for a quick one before giving him the night off.

His quaint Black Country accent is one which you first need to listen to carefully and then go away for half an hour and try to decide what it is he's just said to you. There are distinct benefits to this accent, one being that referees can never tell whether you're being polite or suggesting a new orifice in which they can stuff their whistle.

Equally when negotiating a new contract, the gaffer becomes so exasperated it ends up with Bully typing the contract and he just signs it.

Not only is Bully one of the quickest players in the Football League, he also, due to his physical attributes and fitness, is the one player I would least relish facing on a Saturday afternoon, and strangely enough I happen to know that Bully lives in fear of facing me, but as he is some 4" taller, that's hardly likely to happen.

● ● ● ● ●

Players fortunes in football differ greatly, Mark Hateley a former team-mate and neighbour of mine has gone from rags to riches, and still continues to enjoy a lifestyle which most players envy. Luckily I started at the bottom and liked it, I could have gone to Monaco myself but Birmingham came in in the nick of time.

Another former stable-mate of mine, Gary Gillespie nick-

Who said I'd never lift a cup – I left the saucer on the table though

named 'The Stick Insect' at Coventry found fame and fortune on the treatment table at Liverpool. In fact he's even limped for Scotland a few times. Gary had so much spare time on his hands it enabled him to become a single figure golfer and a mean darts player. In fact Gary was quite mean at everything, the last time he stood a round of drinks Pavarotti had a 28 inch waist.

On the other hand the fortunes of Ian Wallace differed greatly, after being sold from Coventry to Forest for one million pounds he found himself side by side with Eddie the Eagle Edwards, 'on the crest of a slump', and ended up playing in oblivion wherever that is. In fact if I can find out his phone number I'm going to ring him and see if they need a full back!!

● ● ● ● ●

Many players find handling transfer requests a harrowing experience. One such was Irish international Terry Curran (who has had more clubs than I have signed autographs). Terry hit on what he thought to be a failsafe method of dealing with this problem when he wanted to leave Nottingham Forest. He simply produced his request in letter form and handed it to the management. When dealing with a character like Cloughie even the best of us needs to summon up an inner strength to even say good morning. Terry after several deep breaths burst into the manager's office to confront Clough and Taylor after being dropped from the Nottingham Forest side.

"I've had enough," he said and, reaching into his pocket, handed over the letter he said 'explained everything'. Slamming the door behind him and telling the mighty twosome to sort it out, he breezed contentedly up the corridor until he heard those famous Cloughie tones booming: "Young man, get in here now!" He re-entered the room, mystified to be greeted with the comment: "It's true what they say about the Irish. I'm not sorting this out. You can."

Poor Terry had left his angrily written transfer request in his other pocket and instead slapped his gas bill under the great man's nose!

14. Referees

Before we start, let me state here and now, I've got nothing against referees. In fact I quite like them. I couldn't eat a whole one, but I quite like them. After all, they're just like any other normal schizo, usually with more faces than Phil Cool and about as popular as the Poll Tax.

A vast number of the male population have to coax and cajole their wives or girlfriends with promises of undying love and endless supplies of flowers and Milk Tray to get them to dress up in black on a Saturday night. Yet, we have a gaggle of grown men parading in smart black numbers in broad daylight every Saturday afternoon in front of thousands of people who subject them to a never-ending supply of abuse. I'm sure it must be a pre-requisite of a football referee to have spent at least two sessions at Madame Cynthia's Correctional Clinic, although I have to admit I've never seen any there!

So let us pose the million dollar question: What in God's name ever possesses them to do it?

Perhaps they do it for the fame? I know for a fact it's not for fortune. Who likes referees besides me? Certainly not the average supporter because refs are about as popular as a portrait of Jimmy Hill. In fact I wonder why Jimmy didn't become a referee, he always claims to know more about the rules of the game than they do but then, what is there left in life that Jimmy isn't an expert on? There is no doubt he has the physical attributes to take whatever abuse is thrown his way firmly on the chin!

Perhaps I'm being harsh and I don't really wish to generalise but just as in the playing and management side of football, there are the good, the bad (ugly as well) and downright pathetic match officials. At this point, let me introduce you to my memories of Clive (the book) Thomas.

Clive was to football what Hitler was to the Nobel Peace Prize. Clive was the only referee I knew who used to bring a pencil sharpener onto the pitch. At the end of the season he would have more names in his little black book than Joan Collins. I dread to think how he would interpret the new F.A rulings, he'd be sending people off for having bad breath.

Clive's greatest ambition in life was to be the game's main attraction and set his rules accordingly:

Rule 1

Never let a player speak back to you in case he speaks the truth (we never did, we were frightened to interrupt).

Rule 2

Only send somebody off if either there is a large crowd or the TV cameras are there.

Rule 3

Always get your version in the 'News of the World' first.

Rule 4

Always remember the crowd are there to watch you, not the game, so don't disappoint them, be controversial.

Rule 5

Mistakes are what other referees make.

Clive, it appears, stuck religiously to these rules, an example of Rule 4 was explained to me by a current Wolves player, Gary Bellamy, who at the time, was involved in a 'top of the bottom' clash for Chesterfield against Exeter City (makes you envious doesn't it?) It was a real crowd-puller with nothing at stake but a win bonus. Whilst inspecting the pitch before the game, Clive turned to Gary, looked up and said: "You'll be expecting a big crowd today." Gaz looked puzzled. Clive clarified his position by adding: "I always put at least 2,000 on the gate when I'm refereeing." What a big-head!

During the same game, a player questioned one of his decisions and, just before being booked, he was told: "Don't ever question my decisions. I've refereed World Cup games, you know." The player, sensing he may as well get hung for a sheep as a lamb, replied: "yes, but you're still an amateur." Clive was reported to have been none-too-impressed. I would best describe him as the Jeffrey Archer of the football world. Smarmy.

I've heard Clive say recently that he wouldn't cross the road to watch a game. Well, if he changes his mind, let's hope he chooses the M1!

But what about the occasional throwback to the good old days, the days when a misfit from the umpiring world was turned into a half-decent ref. Oh yes, you do occasionally get them. They are few and far between, but they do exist.

My favourite was Roger Kirkpatrick, who cut a dashing figure - short, fat and bald. He moved like a pregnant bear dancing on a barbecue but he remembered that it was a man's game and preferred to communicate directly with the players, rather than through the FA disciplinary committee.

Roger would congratulate you when you scored a good goal (so I'm told) and say bad luck when you made a complete ass of yourself (we spoke frequently). He also understood that most players went into tackles with the intention of winning the ball, but could sometimes arrive a split-second late. To quote Norman Hunter after one of his late-tackle bookings: "I got there as quickly as I could, ref." Even if you did take your opponents' legs away, Roger was okay as long as you gave them back afterwards.

He also had a great sense of humour (he had a full-length mirror in the bedroom). The story goes that, during the 1970s, a famous player whose name it would be indiscreet to reveal (okay, it was Rodney Marsh) didn't agree with one of Roger's decisions. Rodney said: "Ref, can I ask you a serious question?" "Of course you may," Roger replied. "Well," added Rodney, "if I was to call you a b••••••, would you send me off?" "Too bloody right I would," came the reply. "Well, would you send me off if I only thought you were a b••••••?" Roger said: "Well, that's a different matter. I couldn't send you off just for thinking something." "In that case then, I think you're a b••••••!" concluded Rodney — and Roger's booming laugh could be heard all over the pitch.

I remember Roger reffing a testimonial game at Coventry's Highfield Road and, to keep in the spirit of the game, came onto the pitch wearing a curly blond wig. Greg Downs was furious when he realised it was missing. Roger looked like an overgrown cabbage patch kid, but that was him, a good laugh, a good communicator and, though it pains me to say, a damn good referee. I knew I'd remember one sooner or later.

Refs are only human after all and we all make mistakes. One of my favourite refs' gaffes was when I was playing for Coventry against Crystal Palace at Highfield Road. The game was televised. You could always tell when the cameras were there. The players dispensed with the usual stretching exercis-

118

es and massage of the legs before the game, and concentrated on grooming their locks (Alan Brazil used to play darts). The air hung heavy with the smell of Harmony hair spray and Vidal Sasoon Gel for extra hold and, to a man, they would all turn and face the TV gantry when warming up, the keeper never gets a touch. Anyway, Palace were awarded a free-kick 25 yards out. We set up our defensive wall, each of us hoping to God that our dangly bits would survive and not end up as earrings. On this occasion, a Palace player touched it sideways (could have been Ray Wilkins on loan) for Clive 'Million Pounds' Allen to unleash a piledriver (I'm told his piles are improving now). Mercifully, it flew over our nervous wall and over Jim Blyth's outstretched fingers. His arms were still down by his side, but, to be fair to Jim, his fingers were definitely outstretched, as the ball rifled into the top corner of the goal, hit the back stanchion and cannoned out back into play. The referee must have been the only one in the stadium not to see it enter the goal. What made it worse for the Palace fans, we went on to win 3-1. Not all bad refs, are they?

On the second occasion, we weren't so fortunate. It was against Manchester United in the packed and hostile cauldron of Old Trafford. It was a televised game in which no quarter was given and no prisoners taken. United were awarded a free-kick on the edge of our box for the minor infringement of obstruction. It was in fact for using a brick wall by the name of 'Big "Jack the Giant" Dyson' to bring Jimmy Greenhoff to an abrupt halt. The referee raised his arm to indicate an indirect free-kick. Just before the free-kick was to be taken, the ref raised his arm again. We began to wonder if he was in fact a practising member of the 3rd Reich, but he left nobody in any doubt that the kick was definitely indirect. Meanwhile, Jimmy Greenhoff had scraped himself off the floor and his televised hairstyle had been revived by the magic sponge, and he took up a position at the end of our wall in the hope of distracting our defence. Greenhof spun away to leave a gap which Sammy McIlroy found with great precision and the ball whistled straight into the goal. No goal? Wrong! The ref cut a dash,

I couldn't eat a whole one

arm raised pointing to the centre circle with a trail of our players in his wake offering him free membership to Guide Dogs for the Blind Charities and various other unprintable adjectives describing his inability to focus correctly. We lost that game 2-1. I always especially hated to lose in my home city against a club I idolised as a kid. Bloody referees!

One factor which contributes to referees making bad decisions is players who feign injury or use gamesmanship perfected to an art form to influence penalty decisions. The past-master of this trend was Francis Lee, who, since leaving football has made a fortune in business selling toilet paper, it's encouraging to see he started at the bottom to make his mark. He took more tumbles than an acrobat in the Moscow State Circus. If you caught Franny in the penalty area with so much as your bootlace, the show would begin, first a swallow dive, followed by a triple salko. By the time the rolling had stopped, he was through the turnstiles and halfway home. All he was short of was a set of six international judges behind the goal holding up cards showing 5.9, 5.9, 5.8, 5.8, 5.9, 5.1 (the last one was the German judge as usual). Franny was definitely one of the game's characters and a good player. I'm told he is now a successful racehorse trainer. I'd just love to be there when one of his horses falls, gets up, appeals and the crowd shout 'penalty'.

Players, in general, are totally dismayed at the refereeing standards and I cannot believe that a sport of world status in which so much is at stake is still officiated by amateurs. There is nothing more frustrating for a pro player who works at the game six days a week to be subjected to poor decisions made by an amateur who is only part-time. Surely the time has come for a full-time professional body of referees. I don't know, perhaps referees are not of this world, maybe they even had a part in Crossroads. Whatever the reason, they are definitely paddling with only one oar in the water.

One good thing is that they all have a good sense of humour and will realise that if I have said anything bad in this chapter, I was only kidding. And they'll realise that I REALLY do like referees, don't I?

15. Funny Thing About Football

Kevin Costner, look out! I've made it. Or I thought I had. Wolves were marketing a new after-shave and requested my services as a member of the 'cast' for a mock advert to be used as a news item on BBC TV.

How would I approach the role? In a Shakesperian thespian sort of way or as a young-free-and-single fun-seeker? The second choice would obviously mean an awful lot of practice and acting. And where would the shooting be done? On location in Barbados under a coconut tree or how about in California, with me cruising in on the surf with the spray moistening my golden hair? Or maybe even in a French Riviera casino where I would be surrounded by a bevy of beauties rubbing their fingers across my hairy chest between the buttons of my shirt. Please excuse me if the type has become a little shaky at this point but I'm really getting into the rôle.

When I woke up and the cameras actually rolled, I was accompanied, not by a collection of gorgeous girls but by Steve Bull and Gary Bellamy. And we weren't in the Pacific, the Caribbean or on the Mediterranean, we were in the Wolves club shop at the back of Molineux's crumbling North Bank. What a letdown! I could see why Bully and I had been chosen, what with our rugged looks and our massive appeal, but why Gary – I thought they were trying to sell the stuff! Kevin Costner could breathe again.

We were told to report at 12.30pm wearing club track-suits and were greeted by a camera crew who I think had just finished filming One Man And His Dog. What a scruffy lot they were. I'd seen better-dressed wounds.

But the organisation was meticulous. I asked them what they wanted us to say. They replied: "Anything you like" and handed each of us a bottle of the magic splash-on. As the whirring of the cameras began, the presenter asked on air: "What do you think of the new after-shave?" I said: "It's lovely, but I couldn't drink a full bottle." That caused a laugh and they asked if we could just go through it once more, leaving the funny line in. Well, I'm okay when I'm speaking spontaneously, but, give me something to recite parrot-fashion and I'm done for. When I was asked the same question under rehearsed conditions, I stammered the reply: "It's nice but, er, I couldn't eat, I mean drink, a full bottle." Cut!

Needless to say, I didn't give up my day job but I turned on the TV to watch how the 'ad' had turned out. I also had the video on stand-by but I needn't have bothered. I looked a right herbert and they had cut the funny bit out. And, as for payment for this artistic load of hogwash, I received a bottle of the very stuff we were advertising. I gave it straight to my mother-in-law. She shaves more than I do.

● ● ● ● ●

There have been times over the years when I've thought the phrases 'Sod's Law' and 'Murphy's' were conjured up with me in mind. Times when I've thought that if I ever became a member of a marching band, I would get the piano.

One such time was a decade or so ago when I was named Coventry City's Player of the Year. Not by the fans, but by the Coventry Evening Telegraph, whose Sky Blues columnist Neville Foulger awarded points out of ten after each match, with the prize of one year's free use of a Talbot car going to the one with the biggest total come the end of the season.

My steady performances over the season, coupled with the occasional lawn-cutting visit to Neville's house, got me the prize and, before kick-off at the last home game of the season, I was presented with the keys to a 1.5-litre Talbot Alpine. No car, just the keys. The car followed a few moments later and it was brilliant. It had simultaneously revolving wheels, opening and closing doors, seats you could sit in, see through windows, the lot.

I drove into the training ground on the Monday, making sure the big-lettered 'Brian Roberts drives Talbot' logo was in full view of the other players as I parked it. Though I say it myself, the car was gleaming – it should have been, I had spent all day Sunday polishing it. It was the first new car I had ever had and was a world away from the 105,000-mile 1969 Austin 1300 I was able to sell after winning the star prize. With the money I received for the Austin, I bought four new mats and an 'I Like Traffic Wardens' fluffy toy for my Talbot.

After training, manager Gordon Milne told us to go straight

to Highfield Road as there was a buffet lunch arranged for us. There were some Talbot officials present. I thought they must be there to officially thank me and to tell me the car couldn't have gone to a better player. To say they had a certain image to live up to and I typified that image to perfection.

I couldn't believe it when they ushered us onto the pitch, where 15 brand spanking new Solaras were neatly parked side by side.

Two days after I had been presented with my Alpine, Talbot were announcing a deal whereby all the first-team squad received a Solara. And the Solaras were better than my Alpine, fully equipped with automatic windows, sun-roof and power-steering. I couldn't believe it! What's more, the other players' models were to be changed every three months whereas I had to keep mine for a year. There's no justice in the world!

16. Celebrity Squares

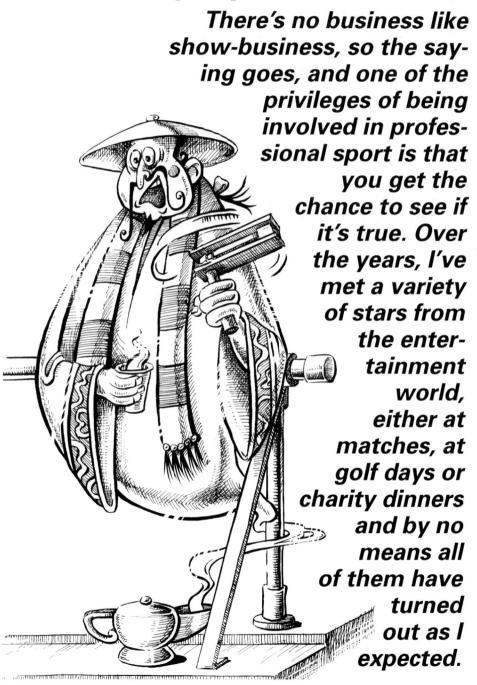

There's no business like show-business, so the saying goes, and one of the privileges of being involved in professional sport is that you get the chance to see if it's true. Over the years, I've met a variety of stars from the entertainment world, either at matches, at golf days or charity dinners and by no means all of them have turned out as I expected.

One such character was Bill Maynard, better known at the time as Selwyn Froggatt. I met Bill at a party given by Jim Blyth at Hinckley and expected at least a couple of 'Magic our Maurice' lines during the course of the festivities. You could have knocked me down with a copy of Ray Wilkins' book on attacking midfield play when Bill turned out to be the true lovey-dovey thespian off stage. He preferred to discuss football matters rather than act the comedian and I was indebted to my wife Alice for waking me up when it was time to go.

The biggest 'Celebrity Squares' coup I can recall though was that of getting the great Mohammed Ali to watch Birmingham City at St. Andrew's. Not even Blues fans do that as a rule! The club must have had the Salesman of the Year on their payroll at the time.

I know Ali - the greatest showman I've ever seen - has suffered a degenerative brain disease since his World Champion days (the first requirement if he ever wants to become a goalkeeper) but somebody must have sold him the best dummy since Burton's closed to get him there. Not that the autograph-hunters minded. As regular visitors to St. Andrew's, they had plenty of empty pages in their books.

We all met Ali after the game and he asked me for my autograph (told you he was sick). Despite his sad problems, he still exuded charisma and great humour and Robert Hopkins indulged in a bit of shadow boxing which nearly ended up with him waking up the following afternoon.

● ● ● ● ●

That's what one or two of the Coventry players probably did after some of our Saturday nights-out a few years earlier. The local Park Lane Nightclub was a regular and popular after-match haunt, largely because the players were allowed in free on production of special passes, which tended to be used several times the same night. The bouncers, who had about as much brains as a fish-cake has meat (don't hurt me lads, I've got two young children and a sick-note from my mum) must

My idea of the perfect balanced diet

have thought we had the biggest squad in the Football League.

Park Lane, owned by a fella called George Henry, a Charlie Endell-type character (from 'Budgie'), had a roped-off cocktail area for visiting celebrities and football stars. I got in on the pretext that I knew Tommy Hutchison. Jim Davidson joined us one night. Jim likes his football as much as he likes getting married and attracted a few funny looks by turning up drastically over-dressed in short-sleeved football shirt, jeans and cap.

My mate Bob Harrison, who had been having a long slow screw up against the wall (that's a pricey cocktail, to the uninitiated), asked Jim to remove the cap. He said it was upsetting the players as they didn't have a cap between them.

Jim saw the funny side and emerged as a sort of likeable rogue. He might have cornered the market in confetti but I've never known one of his ex-wives say a single bad word against him. Well, why say just one when you can say chapters and be paid for it by a Sunday newspaper?

All in all, the stars of sport, stage and screen seem to enjoy the camaradarie in the game and, at the Coventry training ground, we used to see a lot of Danny McAlinden, the former boxer. God knows why! We used to call him Rembrandt because he spent so much time on the canvas.

Another circle in which we seemed to meet celebrities was panto. Either we would go to see them in something like Aladdin or they would come to see us at 3pm on a Saturday. I liked Roger de Courcey the ventriloquist although, as a Crystal Palace supporter, I think he was dafter than his bear. Then there was Cannon and Ball - Tommy Cannon was very down to earth (how else can you be when you've been Chairman of Rochdale?) but Bobby Ball wasn't as friendly as I thought he would be. Nevertheless, he's a very funny bloke. Just ask him. He'll tell you himself.

Overall, fleeting acquaintances with the rich and famous have provided me with some of the highlights of my life in football. Playing the game is the only profession I've had and I never dreamt as I grew up in the back streets of Manchester that I would be rubbing shoulders with the celebrities. It must have been even more exciting for players who had previously had jobs outside the game.

People, for example, like Micky Gynn, who had once earned a living as a hod-carrier for Lego and Terry Gibson, a former station master for Hornby. Not a lot of people know this, but the deal that took Terry to Coventry was just on the point of break-down until the club threw in a Wendy House to clinch his signing.

Then there was Eric Gates, who just missed out on John Hurt's role in The Elephant Man - he was too ugly - and John Sillett, who was sacked from his previous job as a wine-taster because they said he hadn't got the nose for the job. Yes, all of these people have come into football and made their mark, most of them on me.

We have all met celebrities and, at times, been treated like celebrities. Moments like this and chances to see the world in the name of football are moments to cherish. When you're young, you think they will last for ever, but they don't – now I'm trying to hang on in there as long as possible, as you've probably noticed.

I still get a real buzz when I step on to the first tee at a celebrity pro-am golf day, even if the bystanders are asking 'Harry Who?' as my drive roars 75 yards away to the right and into the nearest bunker. Oh well, I can always dream, can't I? And, as Max Boyce might say: "I was there, wasn't I?"

17. Testimonial

Part of the bargain in my record-shattering move from Coventry to Birmingham in 1984 (well, it was the highest fee ever paid by a club beginning with the letter B for a blond right-back with a wife named Alice), was a testimonial.

A match in my benefit between the then present Coventry side and a past Sky Blues side. Or, a past-it Sky Blues side, to be more precise.

Apart from the obvious financial rewards, it was a wonderful opportunity for me to link up again with some of my old buddies from a few years before. Lads like Tommy Hutchison, Ernie Hunt, Willie Carr, Jim Holton and Gary Gillespie.

Tommy Hutch was a great character, a tremendous wit with a caustic tongue. Woe betide any apprentice who answered him back! John Hendrie, a young lad who has gone on to have a flourishing career with Bradford, Leeds, Middlesbrough and Newcastle, once made the mistake of speaking out of turn to Tommy and was subsequently made to go into the first-team dressing-room each morning, stand on the table and sing a song. John would break into verse (Oh Suzanna was Hutch's favourite at the time) and then be told: "Your banjo, John, you're forgetting to play the banjo." Oh, I forgot to tell you. John was completely naked for this ritual, so you can probably guess what the 'banjo' was.

In preparation for my big match, I was also looking forward to seeing Ernie Hunt again. What a character he was! Whenever he was around, there were always stars of stage and screen in his wake . . . Sooty and Sweep, Lassie, Nicholas Parsons and a variety of other top performers.

For years, Ernie pulled a fast one on the coaching staff at Coventry who used to weigh us every Monday morning. We had only to strip down to our underpants before stepping on the scales but Ernie had to be different. He insisted on going the whole hog and being starkers, although the scales were situated in the dining-room within sight of the tea-ladies.

He said he preferred to know his true fighting weight and used to strip off completely before covering his modesty with his hands. And boy, what big hands he had! Unbeknown to the coaches, though, he used to hold the height-measuring pole at the same time as he tipped the scales so, in all the years I knew him, his weight never fluctuated from 10st 3lbs. As his waist-line expanded, I started to think he must be hollow!

Ernie may have been slightly rotund but I never saw him beaten for pace. Not where it mattered anyway - over the first ten yards. He used to argue that that was the only distance that really mattered because it was rare that you had to sprint further than that in a match. What's more, in a bar, Ernie was quicker than Linford Christie.

Ernie always used to be trying something different and will forever be remembered for the donkey-kick free-kick goal in a match against Everton 20 years or so ago. I'm much too young to have been playing that day but I remember it well as I was allowed to stay up late to watch it on Match of the Day.

For younger readers (and this book is probably on the shelves of every primary school library by now), Willie Carr got the ball airborne with a now-illegal flick between his feet and Ernie smashed it on the volley over the Everton wall and into the top corner. It was a goal that was talked about for years and nobody was more surprised than the scorer. The lads 'worked on it in training' but normally the only thing that came off on the practice ground were Ernie's shorts when he wanted to let someone know what he thought of a bad pass.

My testimonial committee stumbled on the idea of re-creating that goal as publicity material for my big game and I managed to contact Willie and Ernie to summon them to Highfield Road for when the cameras started rolling. Willie got the afternoon off from his salesman's post in Wolverhampton and Ernie said the pub in Ledbury could run itself for a few hours.

Come 2.30pm on filming day – the agreed meeting time – the cameras were there, Bob Hall was there (doesn't he wear some dodgy stuff off camera?), Willie Carr was there, my old school mate Bob Harrison was there and the bystanders were there. But where was Ernie? At 3pm, he rolled up, explaining that he'd had a problem with the beer. He hadn't drunk enough of it.

He quickly got changed and trotted out onto the pitch to join us. Ernie was looking portlier than ever. O.K, he was fat, he looked like he'd swallowed a pregnant woman. His No 9 shirt barely fitted over his widening girth, in fact it was tighter

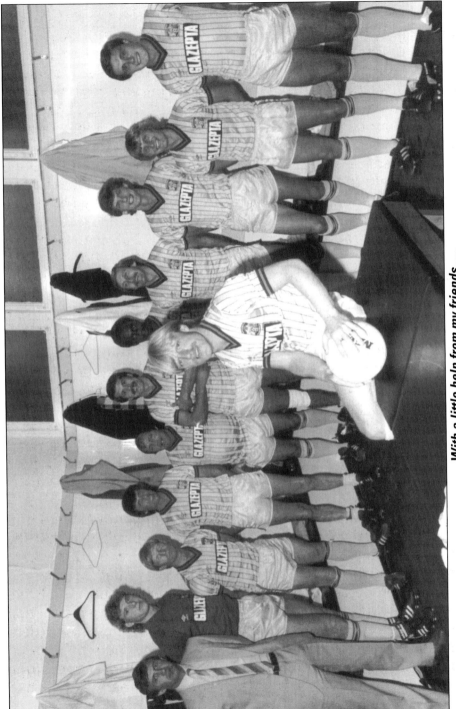

With a little help from my friends .....

than a shark's bum at 40 fathoms. He then suggested a brief warm-up just to make sure the old magic was still there. "On my head, Harry!" he shouted, And, with uncanny accuracy, I hit my cross straight into his stomach. Well, even I couldn't miss that. You've heard of the defence-splitting pass. Well, I'm renowned the Football League for the side-splitting pass.

In the process of Ernie being semi-winded, there was an almighty rip and a moment's silence as we thought he had done himself a severe mischief. Then, the truth dawned as, from beneath his shirt, a velcrose girdle dropped out. It wasn't the only thing that split, though. Our sides went the same way as we doubled up with laughter.

When we regained our composure, Bob Hall shouted "Action" and the cameras rolled. I was in goal, Bob Harrison was the wall (the producers had obviously seen him play before) and Ernie and Willie went into one of football's most famous free-kick routines. Willie flicked the ball up - and Ernie fell over as he tried to shoot. "Cut," shouted Bob Hall. "Take two!" Willie flicked, Ernie volleyed and Bob Harrison held his face in agony as the shot struck him and quickly drew blood. "Cut" - in more ways than one. "Take three!" Willie couldn't flick the ball up. What a shambles. The crew were in danger of breaking their necks as they tip-toed through the undergrowth of discarded film. Eventually, in an effort to avoid the embarrassment of an appearance on It'll be All Right on the Night, I went in the wall and Bob Harrison went in goal. "Take four . . .!"

An hour later, we were still trying and failing. We were broken men, physically and mentally, and quite relieved that the FA had subsequently outlawed the free-kick because the taker was deemed to be having two touches of the ball. At the final attempt, Willie actually delivered the flick beautifully, Ernie connected with a real belter and the ball was just arrowing into the top corner when Bob Harrison flung himself Pat Jennings-like to tip it brilliantly over the angle. The whole fiasco had dragged on so long that Bob, who like me, had stood patiently through numerous aborted takes as the goal had never once been threatened, had forgotten he was meant to let it in.

Ernie questioned Bob's parentage while the director and his crew attempted suicide from the Highfield Road TV gantry. They tried to hang themselves with one of Bob Hall's Billy Smart ties but, fortunately, the elastic broke.

When the whole episode was over, we all agreed we hadn't laughed so much in our lives. And, by the wonders of modern technology, the finished product was brilliant. Everything looked as smooth as clockwork when it was broadcast later, but the viewing public didn't know half the story. Willie flicks ball up, cut, Ernie volleys, cut, ball flies over Bob and me, cut, ball disappears into net, cut. What you can do in the TV industry with a good editor and a tube of super-glue, is nobody's business. They could have made me a world-beater!

●   ●   ●   ●   ●

Come the night of the match itself, the fans were flocking in and I, as the man responsible, was a little concerned about crowd control. Fortunately, they both behaved impeccably. Actually, the ground was full at 7pm - full of empty seats, that is. Apparently there was an unfortunate clash with a party political broadcast and some repeats of the weather forecast on TV. There was virtually only my committee there in the ground and I started to wish I had had a bigger committee. Thank God for the local band King, who offered their services as pre-match entertainment and virtually doubled the attendance. Still, I shouldn't be greedy, anything was a bonus, or so the committee kept telling me.

At least all the players turned up . . . Suckling, Coop, Holton, Gillespie, Roberts, Whitton, Gooding, Carr, Thompson, Ernie Hunt, Steve Hunt, player-coach Powell. What a rogue's gallery. I'd seen better bodies on 1962 Cortinas. George Dalton, the Coventry physio, took one look round our dressing-room and needed a rub-down himself.

Barry Powell gave us the briefest of team-talks. "I've taken a look at the opposition," he said. "I've taken a look at you and this is the best hope we have of winning: Say after me . . . Our Father, who art in heaven . . ."

It might have been an evening for nostalgia and wise-cracks but I was touched by what Gordon Milne wrote in the match programme. "Harry Roberts was Coventry City through and through," he said. "You can't put a price on that sort of player. You would never realise in the transfer market the true worth of a Harry Roberts. His like are the backbone of British football."

Thank-you Gordon, and you're right. No-one ever did realise my true worth. I eventually moved on for £10,000 - a figure more in keeping with a player's signing-on fee, but I mustn't complain. There was the odd perk, like cruising round town in a club Skoda. At first, I misread the small-print of my contract and thought I was being offered club soda. But the chairman told me soda was too expensive - would I settle for a Skoda instead?

Anyway, match-night was here and out we trotted to a rapturous reception from my wife and kids. We were wearing Coventry's yellow and white away strip, which was only slightly less sickly than the late-1970s chocolate brown and yellow, which we used to say made us look like over-ripe bananas. Trevor Peake tossed up with his own personal threepenny bit and I called: "Tails, it never fails." It was heads and Trevor said: "We'll kick into the West End." I replied: "That suits me, my shots always end up there anyway."

Our lads had begun to take the game seriously by this time. Out went the cigarettes, down went the cans of lager, a quick touch of the toes and we were ready. Five minutes later, half our boys were gesturing towards the dug-out for oxygen masks. I think they had peaked too early – in the warm-up. At half-time, by which time we were somehow only one down, there was a mad scramble for the medical table. We let Jim Holton win!

I tried everything I could to motivate the lads before we went back out. "Come on, they'll have the sun in their eyes in the second half (it was a night game), they'll tire later, we've got to show more pride, we've got to put on a good performance for the fans - BOTH of them!" Nothing worked, so finally I relented: "Okay, lads, here's another tenner each." They couldn't get out quickly enough. It was like the start of the Le Mans 24-hour race.

I told you Ernie Hunt was a character. He bandaged his head up for the second half and was carried OUT on a stretcher. He looked like The Invisible Man and had the whole place in fits when he went down 'injured' and, in a pre-arranged stunt, called Maureen from the club offices to bring a reviving gin and tonic out to him on a tray. But, to his credit, Ernie stayed on the full 90 minutes, played a blinder and we emerged with a creditable draw.

● ● ● ● ●

I had two other major testimonial functions, starting with a disco at Coventry's training ground, where King once again played. Boy, they must have been desperate in those days. As a raffle prize, Bob Harrison had managed to get one of Bryan Robson's No. 7 shirts from Ron Atkinson at Manchester United. I spent a fortune on tickets trying to win it as I'd only ever seen the back of it while Bryan sped past me time and time again. I longed to see what the front looked like.

On the evening of the dinner as we got ready at home, I don't know who was the more nervous – me, or Bob, who had to address a distinguished gathering. Here we were, dressed like two penguins with rigormortis, two scruffy-arsed kids who were brought up in Hulme, Manchester, a suburb so downtrodden that Arthur Mullard was the local Avon lady.

Bob promised not to embarrass me. He said my suit had already taken care of that.

We decided to swallow some Dutch courage at the local before heading for the dinner. On arrival at the ground, we were invited into the Directors' Lounge for drinkypoos. Thirteen years I had been at the club and this was my first taste of

Hands up all those who want to be in Harry's team

how the other half lived. Mind you, I made sure it was a good taste!

We were then clapped into dinner which I found quite uncomfortable, but the cream from my doctor cleared it up later.

The speeches were very flattering, so much so I thought I'd turned up at someone else's dinner, though given the money the speakers were receiving it was no wonder. Bob, as per usual, embarrassed me totally by mentioning that being from a family of nine, we were put to bed on pallets and by adding that my Dad was not able to work through having something wrong with his legs – they couldn't walk past pubs!

He was wrong, of course. My Dad did have a job. He was a night repairer of church rooves!

Testimonials, like nostalgia, will soon be a thing of the past. The very idea of players staying at clubs for ten years will be as absurd as expecting a pass from Steve Bull in the penalty area.

Loyalty lasts as long as it takes a player to ring his agent in Marbella and ask if there are any other clubs interested in him. And, if not, why not? If his agent can't be contacted on his mobile phone/car phone/portable phone, then the player will be on to the Sunday papers, then to other clubs and finally to his accountant to see how best he should have the signing-on fee paid to him. No wonder British Telecom are making outrageous profits.

If I sound bitter and cynical about this dubious breed which has attached itself to football, it's only because I am. I really don't see the need for most players to employ them at all.

Okay, if it's someone at the very pinnacle of his career, like Paul Gascoigne, Steve Bull or me, they need someone to handle the many offers they receive from outside the game and to turn the commercial opportunities to their greatest advantage.

But most footballers are bread-and-butter players (bread-and-lard in my case) and need agents as much as George Best needs a home-brew kit for Christmas. They are better off using the players' union, the PFA, to negotiate their contracts for them.

The PFA have trained negotiators to help players get a better deal — and at a fraction of the bill an agent would drop on their door-mat. They're so influential and persuasive they got Bobby Charlton a contract with Vidal Sassoon and then fixed Steve Bull up with a spare-time job as an elocution teacher.

Seriously (and I promise this seriousness won't last long), I know of two players who signed for a First Division club and received signing-on fees of £60,000. One of them had employed an agent to do his negotiating and paid him a princely £12,000 for services rendered. The other employed the PFA for a few hours to do the same job at the rate of £150 an hour. Which one would you choose?

Another example concerned a young First Division player who was negotiating an attractive long-term contract as he neared the end of a particularly impressive season. The manager said he didn't want any agent involved but invited the player to consult the PFA to see if any minor details needed amending.

The player did this and, after a few small amendments, duly signed the contract. The cost of the PFA advice? £400. The cost of his agent? £25,000. Yes, £25,000 — more than most of us earn in a day (told you it wouldn't last long). The agent hadn't actually done anything but had sent the bill in as it was in the small print that he was due a percentage of such agreements. Criminal!

Don't think these goings-on are limited to the big players either. What about the Fourth Division player who was charged £1,000 by his agent for the privilege of accompanying him to the ground of a prospective buying club? No, if you're a player and you're reading this, take my word for it: Stick to the PFA.

By the way, I just happen to be the union delegate at Wolves now, having filled the same post at my previous two clubs, Coventry and Birmingham. At Blues, there were so many disputes arising from wages or bonuses not being paid, that it became virtually a full-time job. Just as well Dave Mackay was manager and I was free most Saturdays — just as he is now!

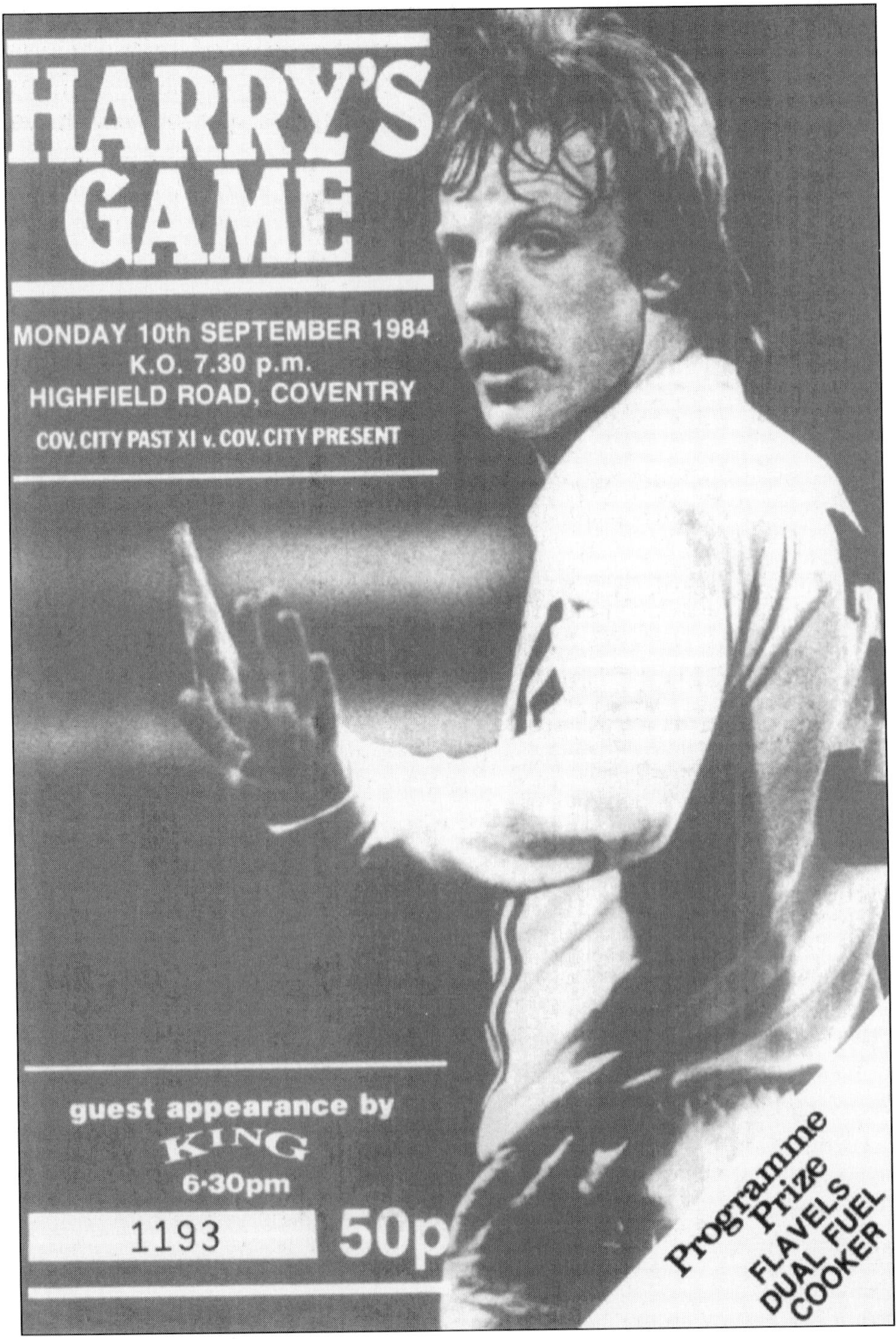

HARRY'S GAME

MONDAY 10th SEPTEMBER 1984
K.O. 7.30 p.m.
HIGHFIELD ROAD, COVENTRY

COV. CITY PAST XI v. COV. CITY PRESENT

guest appearance by
KING
6·30pm

1193   **50p**

Programme
Prize
FLAVELS
DUAL FUEL
COOKER

The only agent I ever want to see as I continue to hop from one pleading club to another in the twilight of my glorious career is the one from Littlewoods who has come to deliver my first divi of £500,000. The only time in my life I will have placed eight crosses perfectly!

18. Building For The Future

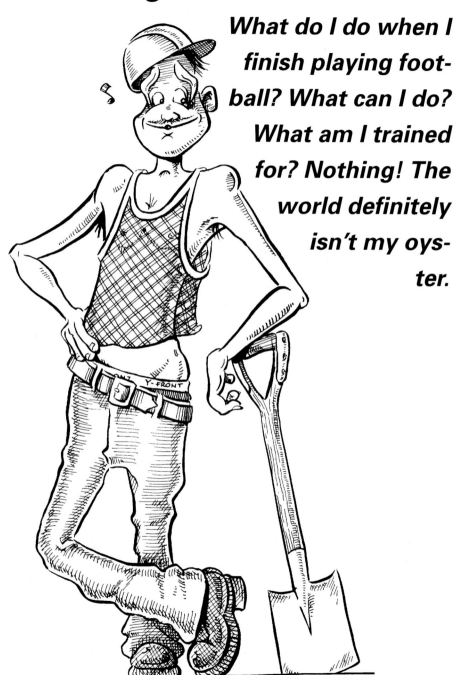

What do I do when I finish playing football? What can I do? What am I trained for? Nothing! The world definitely isn't my oyster.

During my brief spell of unemployment, in between leaving Birmingham in 1990 and signing for Wolves, I signed on at the dole office and was asked about my qualifications. When they told me to fill in the questionnaire, I thought they meant I had to beat up the doorman. Life outside the cosseted world of professional football was threatening to be a bit of a trial.

They asked me again about my qualifications. I told them. They laughed and said: "No, seriously." I said I'd been a professional footballer for over 20 years. They said: "You're suitable for anything unskilled." They'd obviously seen me play.

Therefore, during the close season, I tried my hand in the building industry with a Coventry firm called Beech Construction. Within a few days of my arrival, they were thinking of renaming the company Beech Destruction. To put it kindly, I wasn't a natural. I did get the hang of one or two facets of the job, like wolf-whistling at anything that went past in a dress and pulling my jeans down a few inches to reveal plenty of bum cleavage while I was digging.

They had me digging for two weeks solid. I nearly made it through to Australia. Fortunately, it was a lovely summer and I spent so much time leaning on my shovel that I got blisters on my elbows and sun-burned behind my ears. But I wasn't really cut out for the job. I didn't have the necessary attributes. You had to look like Stan Ogden, drink like Oliver Reed, swear like Princess Anne. Oh, and be able to save money like John Conteh, who claimed a few months ago that he had spent several hundred thousand of his fortune on booze, several hundred thousand on drugs, several hundred thousand on birds and squandered the rest!

My work-mates would be paid on a Friday and, by Monday morning, would be 'subbing' off the gaffer out of the following week's wages. I did my work for nothing - for the experience - and actually ended up owing them money to cover breakages. (This paragraph is included to keep the taxman at arm's length).

After my two weeks on the shovel, the gaffer told me I was in for a rise. I thought he meant more money. He meant it was time for me to get up the ladder and do some roofing. The previous bloke was so mean that he had once been doing some tiling when a 50p piece fell out of his pocket. He was down so quickly to find it that he beat it to the ground and received a painful 50p-shaped cut on the side of his head.

I really enjoyed looking down on people and came to realise what John Bond saw in it! I soon picked up the roofer's language and came out with phrases like: "I can see right down your blouse from here, luv!" I even had a 'Roofers love being on top' sticker on my car.

The lad I worked with was nicknamed Moxey after the character in Auf Wiedersehen Pet. Moxey wasn't the brightest of lads. Rumour had it he had once bought a black and white dog, thinking the license would be cheaper. But, boy, he knew his job. He was up and down the ladder like a trained monkey. He was as thick as a piece of 4 by 2 but had a workrate to match his appetite.

He was one of the skint brigade day in day out, yet, come lunchtime, he would get a 'sub' and head off to the shop to buy three cans of coke, four packets of crisps, two Mars bars and a Curly Wurly. I asked him why he didn't bring sandwiches. He said they made him sick! Mind you, he was always well enough to cadge one of mine.

My lunch box was something to behold. Darth Vader and the rest of the Star Wars cast were on the front, Birmingham City stickers covered the back. I didn't half get some funny looks as well at my first meal-break. My wife had really done me proud - half a chilled melon, two prawn and mayonnaise wholemeal sandwiches from Marks & Spencer (the lads thought I had got sand in my luncheon meat butties) and an energy-reviving isotonic Lucozade. Well, we professional athletes have a quietly-spoken, well-groomed, church-going image to live up to. Here I go again, sounding like Billy Graham, and with my nose starting to grow. Needless to say, by the end of the first week, I was on corn beef sarnies with the rest of them, washed down with a can of shandy.

It was good, clean, honest eight-till-five work. Something I

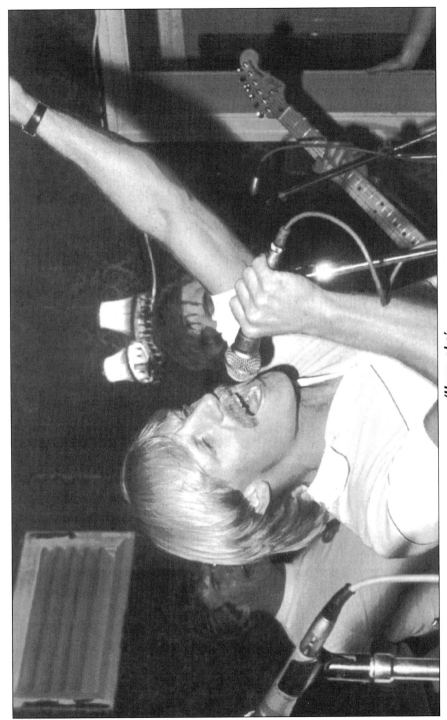

'Harry-oke'
And they said I was no good at the Blues!

wasn't at all used to. The eight-till-five bit I mean, not the good, clean, honest aspect. I had been more of a ten-till-twelve man for more years than I cared to remember, with a couple of hours feet-up time in the afternoon. Life on the site really did open my eyes. I'm usually a bit of an insomniac but I had no trouble sleeping during my 'Destruction' days.

I also developed the best tan of my life. I told all the lads back at Blues that I'd been to the Bahamas for my holiday. Mind you, I had some trouble explaining away the sight of me in hob-nail boots and big overalls on all my photographs.

By the way, the next time you're booking a holiday, take the trouble to find out when we're reporting back for pre-season training. I guarantee that these few days are always the hottest of the year. In 20 years, I can only remember it raining once - I'm sweating just thinking about it. Nobody in their right mind would say they look forward to this torture. Slogging your way back to fitness after the summer break is the scourge of we professional footballers' lives.

I must say, though, that the building work prepared me nicely for the hard graft this one year. I felt great for two and a half weeks, then I pulled a muscle and I was out for the next four!

The next time I do hod carrying for my holidays, I'll make sure it's on a site where they are building bungalows.

A lot of my past colleagues have either gone into the insurance business or have become landlords. I can only assume that some of the voluntary work they put into the License trade in their playing years, as well as a considerable part of their remuneration, was, in fact, an investment for their future outside football.

Personally, I can only ever see the fun in being the other side of the bar. However, both Jim Blyth and Jim Holton have managed to follow on from their professional careers and still keep their good looks. At this point, I wish to make it clear that I'm not subject to any form of bribery or, in the case of Big Jim Holton, intimidation.

So what will I do next? Well, I can assure you that I will, as always, put 100 per cent into my next job, just as I have always done. And, if any kids fail to use the Green Cross Code correctly whilst using my crossing, they'll feel the sharp end of my lollipop stick.

In Print

Apart from his regular columns in the Sports Argus, Harry's humour has featured in some other publications....

Questions & Answers

Harry Roberts has been put under the spotlight for the fans twice in matchday programmes, first in October 1985 by *Blues News,* later by *Molinews* in January 1991.

Q If there was one footballing wish that could be granted, apart from the obvious FA Cup Final appearance what would it be?

A To score the winning goal in a practice match without the boss disallowing it.

Q What other sports do you play and how well?

A Golf — my biggest problem is standing too close to the ball, after I've hit it.

Q When you're out on the pitch in the thick of the action are you aware of supporters shouts or are you too busy to notice?

A I only hear the boss disputing the existence of my father.

Q What car would you like to own if you could afford it and if you have passed your test, how many attempts did it take?

A A Reliant Robin — the last one I had, I caught a rat dragging it down Hagley Road.

Just the once but it took a few times.

Q Do you read, if so what kind of books do you prefer, and which authors?

A I generally borrow Stevie Wonder's, I've got blis-ters all over my fingers.

Q Looking ahead, what career would you like to pursue when your playing days are over?

A I wanted to be a doctor, but I didn't have the patients.

Q If Jim could fix it for you, what treat would you ask for?

A To be like him and present a cheque for £10,000 to the unknown soldier's mother.

Q Where was your best ever holiday and when?

A Thailand — 1982.

Q When you were younger did you have a foot-balling hero? Who was he? Have you since met him and if so where?

A George Best — Yes — Coventry City v Northern Ireland.

Q How do you spend the rest of your day after training?

A Looking for somebody who wants my auto-graph.

Q Outside of sport, do you have any hobbies?

A Watching my wife gardening and D.I.Y. My wife says: "Put up a shelf", and I say: "Do-It-Yourself".

Q If you were host of a Wogan-type chat show who would you invite to interview?

A Erika Roe, just to keep a breast of the times.

Q What or who makes you laugh?

A Gary Newbon's Book of Football Sincerity.

Q Are there any other member of your family involved in football, if so could you give details?

A My brother John, he does the Pools.

Q Your house is on fire, everyone is safe and you have a few moments to rescue one of your possessions. What would it be and why?

A The Family Allowance Book and twenty-five yard swimming certificate.

Q If you were to visit that famous desert island what would your personal choice of eight records be?

1 – Matchstick Men, Status Quo.

2 – Funky Street, Arthur Connolly.

3 – High Ho Silver Lining, Jeff Beck.

4 – The Town I Love So Well, Paddy Reilly.

5 – All Night Long, Lionel Ritchie.

6 – Sultans Of Swing, Dire Straits.

7 – Spirit in the Sky, Norman Greenbaum.

8 – Love On The Rocks — Kermit the Frog.

Q They say gentlemen prefer blondes .. what is your preference, blonde or brunette?

A Like the mother-in-law Platinum blondes with dark roots.

Q What has been your most embarrassing moment, either in or out of football?

A Being mistaken for a full-back, that's the last time I invite Ray Charles to a game.

Q Some people hate being stuck in long queues. What do you find most annoying?

A People complaining about being stuck in long queues.

When quizzed by *Molinews,* the following answers were forthcoming.

Name: Brian Lesley Ford Roberts (better known as Harry)

Age: 22 ¾

Date of birth: 6.11.55 B.C. (before contraceptives)

Place of birth: Manchester

1. What is your idea of perfect happiness?

Finding anybody who hasn't heard my jokes.

2. Which living person do you most admire?

Elvis Presley

3. Which footballer do you most admire?

George (hic) Best

4. What is your favourite pastime?

Looking for someone who wants my autograph

5. What do you most dislike about yourself?

My uncanny resemblance to Robert Redford and my modesty

6. What do you most dislike in other people?

Inability to recognise my obvious talent.

7. What is your greatest fear?

Being transferred back to Birmingham

8. What is your happiest memory?

When Stevie Wonder said I was the best full-back he'd ever seen

9. Who are your favourite musicians?

Wonderstuff and Pop Will Eat Itself

10. What would be your motto?

This time next year I'll be a millionaire

11. How would you like to be remembered?

As a footballer not a journalist — everyone says to me "oh you write that column in The Argus — but you don't play any more do you?"

12. What gets you depressed?

Bank statements

13. What is your favourite journey?

Coming off the bench

14. Which talent would you most like to have?

Bo Derek

15. When, if ever, do you lie?

See age above

16. What is your favourite sport other than football?

Solo synchronised swimming, with my nose clips off

17. What is the best game you've ever played in and why?

The League Cup semi-final first leg for Coventry against West Ham. We won 3-2 and were only 90 minutes from Wembley. Unfortunately we lost 2-0 in the second leg.

18. What is the best game you've ever seen?

Manchester United winning the European Cup at Wembley in 1968.

19. What one thing would you like to change about football?

Defenders getting more credit

20. If you weren't in professional football, what would you most like to do?

Be Bully's agent.

AND SO, WE BID A FOND FAREWELL TO THE MAN WHO HAS SOMETIMES SINGLE-HANDEDLY KEPT US ENTERTAINED.

GOOD LUCK AND BEST WISHES FOR THE FUTURE, HARRY.

BY MY RECKONING, THE HARRYTHON REACHED 824 MINUTES, SO PLEASE SEND YOUR MONEY TO ME IF YOU SPONSORED HIM, ADE